J. P. Stern was born in Prague and was educated there and at St John's College, Cambridge. During the war he served in the Czech Army and the Royal Air Force.

He was for many years Fellow and Tutor of St John's College and Lecturer in the department of German at Cambridge. Since 1972 he has held the Chair of German at University College London, and he is Honorary Director of the Institute of Germanic Studies, University of London. He has been Visiting Professor at the City College of New York, the University of California at Berkeley, the State University of New York at Buffalo, the University of Virginia at Charlottesville, Göttingen University and at Cornell University, Ithaca, NY.

Among Professor Stern's publications are *Ernst Jünger: a writer of our time* (1952), *G. C. Lichtenberg: a doctrine of scattered occasions* (1963), *Re-Interpretations: seven studies in nineteenth-century German literature* (1971), *On Realism* (1972), *Hitler: the Führer and the People* (1975), *A Study of Nietzsche* (1979) and, with M. S. Silk, *Nietzsche on Tragedy* (1983).

Modern Masters

Nietzsche

J. P. Stern

Fontana Press

First published in 1978
by Fontana Paperbacks,
8 Grafton Street, London W1X 3LA
Second impression, August 1979
Third impression, October 1981
Fourth impression, with minor revisions,
in Fontana Press, May 1985

Set in Linotype Pilgrim
Made and printed in Great Britain by
William Collins Sons & Co. Ltd, Glasgow

In Memoriam
Werner Brock
28 March 1901 - 21 June 1974

Contents

Acknowledgements

I am grateful to the Rockefeller Foundation and to my own College for making it easy for me to write this essay: the former by inviting me to the Villa Serbelloni, their study centre at Bellagio above Nietzsche's beloved Lake Como, where I enjoyed such magnificent hospitality as Nietzsche on his restless wanderings never knew; the latter by granting me a term's sabbatical leave to complete the work.

For permission to reprint, thanks are offered to the editors of *The Journal of European Studies*, *Encounter* and *Nietzsche: Imagery and Thought* (ed. J. M. S. Pasley and published by Methuen), in whose pages different versions of parts of Chapters 3 and 7 are to be found.

Having consulted and made use of the available translations (see p. 159), I decided to offer my own versions of quotations from Nietzsche's works. As on previous occasions, I am deeply grateful to Sheila Stern for help in revising them. Nietzsche's writings, especially those published posthumously, abound in typographical emphases; I have used italics only where not to have done so would have altered his meaning.

I am happy to acknowledge my gratitude to my friend Chris Waller, who offered countless suggestions on how my text might be improved, and helped generously to establish references and quotations, especially from the new and as yet uncompleted critical edition of Nietzsche's work.

J.P.S.
University College London
July 1977

Abbreviations

1 Nietzsche in Company

I

Friedrich Nietzsche belongs among those very few thinkers
– Karl Marx and Sigmund Freud are the others – whose
standing as modern masters is undoubted: had they not
lived the life of modern Europe would be different.
Among all the other modern masters they are unique:
the influence of their speculative thinking touches on
every aspect of our experience. Marx died in 1883,
Nietzsche's work was over by 1889, Freud died in 1939.
There are no biographical connections between them
(apart from the fact that Freud knew, and admired, some
of Nietzsche's psychological views). All three are part of
our nineteenth-century inheritance – our inheritance from
an age which, more than any other, believed in ideas, and
in change, reform and revolution through the power of
ideas.

All three were intellectuals with a deep desire for *concrete* change, thinkers who, for a time at least, turned
ideologists. Their work, unlike that of their philosophical
predecessors, is in no sense disinterested. The aim of their
thought was to uncover a secret concealed in men's minds;
these minds they wished to change, and with them the
world. They saw their undertaking as the solving of a
secret, and all opposition to it as a conspiracy: a conspiracy of men with vested social and material interests,
thought Marx; of men with vested moral and religious
interests, thought Freud; of men who choose to be only
half alive and resent the few who live generously and
dangerously, thought Nietzsche. Formulating their fore-
casts in a language designed to make them come true,

they took little trouble to separate their findings from their intentions. They made a number of confident prophecies, yet the full consequences of their philosophical undertaking escaped them.

All three were professed atheists who looked on the belief in God as an historically determined symptom of man's weakness and subordination. They offered to liberate him from that belief, partly by demonstrating its illusoriness, partly by fostering as its alternative various forms of self-reliance and self-assertion. Characteristically – and here one must go by the style as well as the message of what each wrote – only Nietzsche shows an awareness of the full significance of the loss of religious belief in our experience.

They tended to underestimate what they owed to their age. They were not always aware of the extent to which their own historical situation formed what Nietzsche called 'the horizon' of their thinking, yet this – their historicity – is precisely part of the fascination and interest they have for us. Thus all three identified 'scientific' with systematic knowledge; both Marx and Freud aimed at a rhetoric and terminology derived from the natural sciences: theirs, we can see, are characteristic nineteenth-century preoccupations, yet only Nietzsche recognized them as such.

Each directed his thinking toward a single leading idea which can be briefly stated (and has often been misstated) – an idea which was to unlock the secret of all that men do: and in each case this explanation proceeds by way of *what makes men* do what they do. None of these three modern masters respects the distinction, fundamental to the liberal mind, between what a thing is and how it came to be what it is; but, equally, none is eager to apply his explanation to his own work.

These leading ideas are: motivation through material

interest; sexual motivation; the will to power. In each case, the motive in question is seen as the begetter of value judgements and therefore (so the argument runs) not subject to them. For as long as it dominates the mind, each of these leading conceptions is said to exclude all impartial insights and stable, 'objective' knowledge. Conversely, as soon as 'Erkenntnis' (which in German is always a dynamic mode of knowledge) is initiated, the ensuing explanation becomes an explaining away. These are passionate thinkers. Just as there is something parricidal in their attitude toward the past, so there is something suicidal about their conceptual schemes: each time, the thinker is excluded from the thought he has created.

Is it a coincidence that all three were German? But perhaps we had better ask first, How German were they? Marx was an emancipated Rhenish-Prussian-Jewish intellectual who spent most of his life in exile; Nietzsche, a German (Bismarck moustache and all) on any reckoning save his own, claimed Polish aristocratic ancestry, came to think the foundation of the Second Reich in 1871 an unmitigated disaster, and returned to Germany only when his work was done and his mind was spent; and Freud was a Moravian German-speaking doctor of orthodox Jewish background, who would have lived all his life in Imperial Vienna had not another quasi-Viennese provincial sent him into exile, to die, like Karl Marx, in Hampstead. They are hardly very representative Germans, yet they all belong to one tradition, one Germany of the mind. They have their intellectual roots in a culture whose dynamic quality Nietzsche saw reflected in its very language: whereas 'reality' derives from 'res' and 'realia', a static concept, (he writes[1]) 'Wirklichkeit' derives from the dynamic 'wirken', 'to affect by working on . . .'

But it was, for them, a spiritual and intellectual dynamism. When Bertolt Brecht, half a century after Nietzsche's death, observed that 'With us everything slips all too readily into the impalpable and disembodied – we start talking about a *Weltanschauung* after the world itself has dissolved', adding that 'With us, even materialism is abstract',[2] he was pointing to a disposition of mind which Marx, Nietzsche and Freud viewed ambivalently and critically, yet which they fully shared. The culture into which they were born largely ignored social questions; viewed with uneasy distaste the commercial and industrial successes of the world that sustained it; favoured a picture of 'reality' which offered little resistance to fundamental speculation; and looked on intellectual revolution as a substitute for social and economic change. The scheme of values by which this culture was sustained – a scheme challenged by all three men – put the highest premium on the life of the mind.

Nietzsche came to dislike the consequences of Germany's victory in the Franco-Prussian War of 1871 because he saw the new Reich as the politicization and 'extirpation of the German spirit', whereas he believed that Germany's true mission in the world should be non-political and cultic, indeed mythopoeic. The spirit she should follow was to be not the spirit of Sedan but of pre-Socratic Greece. (Incidentally, the love of classical Greece was not the least of the gifts all three men derived from their common native tradition.) He distrusted excessive intellectuality. He certainly did not share Freud's belief that all the necessities to which men in society are prey could one day be reduced to, and perhaps solved as, problems of the individual mind. He was more inclined to view abstract arguments the way Marx viewed them (when they were not his own) – as rationalizations of desires and gratifications which had nothing to do with 'the pursuit of knowledge for its own sake'. Yet it is impossible to overlook that middle-class unity of intellectual concerns which all three men shared. It was a single yet complex spirituality which, at the cost of political tutelage and social fetishism,[8] created the most scholarly and intellectual culture modern Europe has ever known; and also, as it turned out, the most vulnerable. To all the phases of the history of this culture Nietzsche's writings provide a brilliant critical commentary.

There is irony in the fact that all three men saw it as part of their programme to prove the illusoriness of morality. To have told them that what informs their thinking is a deep moral concern would have elicited little but contempt (from Marx), disdain (from Nietzsche), and an ironical shrug (from Freud). Yet this, ultimately, is the most important thing they share: anguish at the fragmentation of men's lives (Z II § 20) and a moral care for the future of mankind. Marx's critique of the consequences of the division of labour, Nietzsche's horror of history seen as an endless Golgotha of betrayals and revenge born of resentment, Freud's pessimistic critique of the etiology of civilization – these are signs of their common concern with what had once been called 'the whole man'. This is the end for which Nietzsche's Superman and Marx's classless society are conceived. These fabulous constructs have no equivalent in Freud; but then, who has ever heard of an Austrian utopia . . .

II

No sooner have we set out the common ground of our three 'masters' than it becomes obvious that each of the affinities mentioned needs qualifying. Certainly Nietzsche's place in this company is highly problematic. He cannot, least of all in the heyday of Schopenhauer, Schelling and Hegel – the great metaphysical system-makers – be seriously presented as a systematic thinker. The doctrine of 'the will to power' does not occupy the central position in his thought that the doctrine of motivation by material interest occupies in Marx's scheme, or the doctrine of sexual motivation in Freud's. Nietzsche's notes and plans toward a systematic philosophy belong to the last phase of his active life, the period from *c.* 1884 to 1888. These attempts are important, yet they remain fragmentary. They are not the crowning achievement of his thinking, though he certainly intended them as such. His writings are too rich and too varied to be brought under one common rubric. The writer makes rings round the thinker.

Little of what Marx and Freud wrote stands before us as the work of a free intelligence, without its harness of system. Each writes, not to induce thought and the freedom of thought, but to convince, even to bludgeon into conviction. Diverse facts are assembled for the purpose of definition, definitions are compressed into a technical terminology whose chief virtue is 'scientific' stability and whose chief function is to be available, without further recourse to the world of facts, in the next chain of arguments. Hence Marx's and Freud's tedious habit of referring the reader confidently from one work to supporting passages in earlier works which then turn out to be less than confidence-inspiring. Hence, too, the mastership, the massive strength of their thought, and the relatively undistorted influence they have exercised upon their followers.

Nietzsche, however, even though he has a consistent point of view, is forever setting out on new beginnings. Of the three, he is the only one who strives for unlimited consciousness. With this goes the fact that he is incomparably the most literary of modern philosophers (literary *as* a philosopher; not, like Sartre, a philosopher writing fictions); and his literary debt is European in scope. The appearance of new beginnings is not only part of the literary effect he aims at. It also reflects his unabating care to remain free from the influence of others and from the fetters of his own prejudices – and this concern, in a writer whose every observation is shot through with value judgements, to the faithful reader constitutes a perpetual challenge. In the freedom and variety of intellectual experiment lies Nietzsche's real consistency. What he is concerned with is 'only' a speculative freedom, but as such it is the existential condition of a man whose life is given over wholly to speculation. This freedom, we shall see, can be both joyous and terrifyingly bleak.

The overwhelming impression he leaves with us is not one of subtlety, or lightness of touch, or richness of reference, or consideration for his reader (though he is capable of all these). It is an impression of intellectual energy. To read him is exhilarating for the adventure of sharing the reflective force manifest in almost every formulation and new thrust at a problem. Another name for this energy is truthfulness, even though his questioning is directed not only at the truth of this or that statement or belief (of his own or of other men's), but at the function and value of truth itself.

Nietzsche's is essentially a modern kind of truthfulness. Experiencing the world as a fragmented thing, he conveys it as such; unmasking all notions of 'Being' as mere myths, he settles for 'reflections', notes, informal witnesses of discontinuous 'becoming'. In this sense he seems more truthful – and more modern – than Marx, who disguised the discontinuities of his thought (which were not so very different from Nietzsche's) by thrusting a system over them. Yet Marx's work, too, remains a torso; it was not he who gave it the name of 'dialectical materialism'. The diversity of his insights, too, is revealed in the sheer unevenness and undirected intellectual energy of his style.

The leaps and strange balances of Marx's rhetoric – its unexpected metaphors and violent inversions, the effect of words on the page which do not accumulate to confirm one another, each articulation superseding and challenging the one before[4] – all this is more accurately prophetic of *our* kind of discourse, more *like* Nietzsche's anticipations, than Marxists have ever seen fit to acknowledge.

Nietzsche was not much of a practitioner of 'the will to power'; he only described it. Occasionally he likes to strike heroic attitudes, but really he is defenceless. We wonder how, questioning and undermining every view – almost *because* it looks like providing a stable answer – a man can sustain thought and life itself; and Nietzsche wonders too :

> I do not wish for life again. How have I borne it? Creatively. What makes me bear the sight of life? The view of the Superman who affirms life. I have tried to affirm it myself – alas! [*WKG* VII/1 p. 139]

(This is written in 1882-3, at the time of *Zarathustra*, the most 'life-affirming' of all his books.)

He believes in the possibility of a system that would not be a betrayal of individual truths :

> It would have to be something that was neither subject nor object, neither force nor matter, neither spirit nor soul : but shall I not be told that such a thing will resemble nothing so much as a phantasmagoria? I too believe it will – all the better for that! Of course, it must resemble that and everything else which exists or could exist, and not only a phantasmagoria! It must have that dominant family likeness by virtue of which all that is, recognizes itself as related to it. [*WKG* VII/3 p. 376]

But what he doubts is whether 'the age' is capable of such a system, and whether *he* is, knowing himself to be part of his age.

This historicizing reversal of Nietzsche's thought is characteristic. What others have seen as a fundamental or 'perennial' problem in epistemology or ontology or logic, he will dismantle into psychological or historical consideration – into 'not yet', or 'no longer', or 'not this man'. His choice, therefore, 'in these circumstances', 'in this brave century of mine', is for freedom of new beginnings and for clarity of expression. From the most casual notebook entry to the image-studded *art nouveau* rhetoric of *Zarathustra*, he is incapable of obscurity (lapses of taste and mistakes of tone are a different matter). And yet, like Hamlet – 'were it not that I have bad dreams . . .' – the impression he leaves is not that of a free man.

The spheres of personal experience, philosophical venture and literary expression all meet in the question of Nietzsche's freedom. He chooses to be as free from the obligations of society (of family, class, nation, profession) as a man can be – a man who retains a deep longing for friendship, for a public, and for disciples, too. He forces the circumstances – including his health, his temperament, the failure of his professional prospects – to force the choice on him. This is his *amor fati*, the experience of life he chooses his philosophizing to reflect. And since this experience has provided him with amazingly little insight into any form of institutionalization – political, social or national – how can the arguments of his books be other than unsystematic, unspecialized and unconfined, a unique free venture? And again, choosing a mode of writing as free as possible from the restrictions imposed by more extended literary forms, he recognizes the historical situation reflected in his choice: 'The only thing that can nowadays be well made, that can be a masterpiece, is the small thing. Only in that is integrity still possible.' [CW 2nd postscript]

What is this 'nowadays', this 'fatality of being modern'? What are Nietzsche's bad dreams? He is almost a free man. Perhaps he could be entirely free – he certainly believes he could be – were he not tormented by the thought that 'God is dead', and by the thought that men behave as though they 'had not yet heard the news that "God is dead".' [Z introduction] That lurid metaphor, 'the death of God', sets the limits to his freedom; is the horizon that encircles his speculative life, which is his life.

III

'Mad genius . . . evil Teuton . . . satanic mind' were words applied by a respectable critic to Nietzsche when I first wrote about him more than twenty-five years ago. The atmosphere which provoked those irate remarks no longer prevails, but now his writings are threatened by an opposite danger – that of being read as though he were a cool, systematic philosopher or a poet needing his symbols counted and his images classified; his relationship to twentieth-century totalitarian politics is either denied or ignored. These oscillations are not surprising. His work is the seismograph of modern Europe.

Nietzsche's reputation in Germany between the two wars, and in France and England since the Second, has been that of an existential thinker. This is a wide term but not a vague one. It means (among other things) that a particularly close relationship obtains between Nietzsche the man and Nietzsche the philosopher; a relationship as close as that between D. H. Lawrence the man and Lawrence the novelist. Nor is this a gratuitous comparison, seeing how much of the Laurentian spirit is in fact Nietzschean: 'I have at all times written my work with my whole body and my whole life' – this is Nietzsche writing, not Lawrence – 'I don't know any "purely intellectual problems" . . . These things you know as your thoughts, but your thoughts are not your experiences.' [*WKG* V/1 p. 644] And when Zarathustra acts as Nietzsche's mouthpiece (for example Z II § 2), he loudly proclaims the message of 'commitment' as the identity of thinking and willing and being. It is this 'Nietzscheanism' which is extolled in W. B. Yeats's lines,

> God guard us from those thoughts men think
> In the mind alone;
> He that sings a lasting song
> Thinks in a marrow-bone

– lines which hide one of the chief intellectual superstitions of our age. Why thought that is less 'committed' should be inferior is not explained.

The dubious nature of this doctrine of heroic commitment did not escape Nietzsche himself. He reflects on the vulgarity of minds that will take nothing less than the personal witness (replete with sores and suffering) as evidence for the truth of an opinion; mercifully, at the point where such insistence is apt to become a bore he, unlike his disciples, is quite capable of an ironic disengagement: 'But let's leave Herr Nietzsche! What concern of ours is Herr Nietzsche's health?' [*CW* introduction § 2] Again, he invokes this disengagement when commending *The Will to Power* as 'a book for *thinking* and nothing else – it belongs to those who take *pleasure* in thinking and nothing else' [*Mus* XIV pp. 373 f]: yet this pleasure has no other source than those 'purely intellectual problems' he had condemned as inauthentic . . . How 'authentic', then, is this image of the heroic thinker (perpetuated

23

in a hideous bust by Max Klinger, but also in Nietzsche's own Prussian self-stylizations when he poses for a photograph), committed with all his being to each thought of his great reflective venture?

In a sense it is not true at all. In the sense with which we must be concerned much of the way, Nietzsche's thinking is a series of experiments 'which I live' [*WP* § 1041] – some of them tentative speculations, hunches and suspicions which come and go, some of them *in corpore vili*. 'I desire that your hypothesizing should reach no further than your creative will,' [Z II § 2] Zarathustra calls to us: are we to think that Nietzsche obeys Zarathustra's command in that notorious reflection in which he rejoices in Galiani's observation that predictions are apt to be self-fulfilling, that 'pre-vision is the cause of European wars', and then adds, 'Since I do not share the [anti-war] views of my friend, the late abbé Galiani, I am not afraid to predict and therefore conjure up the causes of wars'? The relish expressed in such images of violence as 'the blond beast' [*GM* I § 11] is undeniable. The best we can say for their author is not that he is living out 'the reality behind the words', but that he is conducting experiments in words and ideas, and *trying out* what their effect might be. His brilliant versatility is unthinkable without a dose of histrionics. In his bitter attacks on Richard Wagner, on Wagner's insincerity and religiosity, Nietzsche seems to be looking for art without artifice, opera without operatic effects, for theatre without theatricality – yet he would be the last to deny that there is, not indeed insincerity, but role-acting and conscious deliberation in his own changes of style and modulations of tone and all the other devices which make his prose such incomparable pleasure to read. Besides, where commitment to a chosen task is concerned, who will say whether Wagner's or Nietzsche's is the more intense, the more authentic and 'heroic'? Wagner loved to boast of his loneliness and suffering. Perhaps there were times when Nietzsche too did not feel the indecency of such weight-lifting contests, when he did not mind it enough.

However that may be, in another, more comprehensive sense the existential claim is true: to his philosophic venture Nietzsche's entire life is dedicated, and every comfort and consolation is sacrificed. However, a man's capacity for sacrifice is not in itself a value. The experience which divides us from Nietzsche makes us reject a penitential ethic which determines 'the order of men's rank' according to their capacity for suffering [*JS* end]. Nor can strenuousness be a value for us. What we acknowledge is not the heroic stance, not a self-created value, but the strange aura that surrounds Nietzsche's venture. It is an aura of grave, Hamlet-like charm – the charm that belongs to every tragic character. It derives from the knowledge, which Nietzsche shares with Hamlet, of being over-taxed by his chosen task.

Thomas Mann in his Nietzsche essay of 1947 speaks of the boy's and adolescent's prim and exemplary normality; the early letters and reports show his eagerness for learning, his immense intellectual gifts, his gentle gravity. The role of destructive critic did not come easily to him, nor the role of stentorian prophet. In doing verbal violence to a world he diagnosed as decadent he had to do violence to his own nature. Did he *choose* the moment 'when he himself might his quietus make'? Yet he decided to love his fate. Perhaps the moment he chose was the moment when he knew that he had done all it was given to him to do.

Any attempt at a coherent interpretation of writings so hybrid and at times so contradictory in content, and so remarkably versatile in form, is bound to be problematic.

2 A Chronology of Nietzsche's Life

1844

15 October: Nietzsche born in Röcken in Saxony. Christened Friedrich Wilhelm (after the King of Prussia) by his father, a Lutheran pastor. Nietzsche's mother was the daughter of a Saxon country vicar. On both sides of his family Nietzsche came from a long line of Lutheran clergymen.

1846

10 July: Elisabeth, his only sister, is born.

1849

30 July: father dies as the result of brain injury; or of a congenital disease of the brain?

1850

The family moves to Naumburg.

1852

Nietzsche moves from the local elementary school to a private preparatory school and then to the Naumburg 'Domgymnasium'. Mixes very little with others. In 1856 the boy is absent from school because of severe headaches and pain in the eyes.

1858

In a diary, recalls his beginnings as a composer and reviews his literary productions (some 50 poems).

1858–64

Attends Schulpforta, Germany's most famous Protestant boarding-school. Receives a brilliant classical education. Is confirmed in 1861. His health continues indifferent. With two friends he founds Germania, a society devoted to the study of the arts.

1864

October: matriculates as classical scholar in the University of Bonn. Joins a student corporation, Franconia.

1865

February: Nietzsche taken to, and flees from, a Cologne brothel. Deussen (friend and famous Indologist) later comments: 'mulierem nunquam attigit' [he never touched woman].

Moves with Ritschl (one of his professors at Bonn) to Leipzig. Discovers the philosophy of Schopenhauer. Beginning of friendship with fellow-classicist, Erwin Rohde.

1866

Rewrites (and publishes in 1867) various learned essays, including his study of *Theognis*.

1867

9 October: begins military service in a cavalry company.

1868

March: chest injury while mounting a horse.
October: returns to Leipzig full of doubts about 'the philological brood ... its mole-like activities ... their indifference to the true and urgent problems of life' (to Rohde, 20 November).
November: first meeting with Richard Wagner.

1869

February: nominated Extraordinary Professor of Classical Philology at Basle.
May: first visit to Wagner and Cosima von Bülow at Tribschen. First meetings with the historian Jakob Burckhardt.

1870

April: nominated full Ordinary Professor.
From August: serves as volunteer medical orderly in Franco-Prussian War.

Friendship with Franz Overbeck, church historian and atheist. Expresses feelings of revulsion for the ethos of his profession: 'No entirely radical truth is possible [in the universities]' (to Rohde, 15 December). Nietzsche conscious for the first time of a great personal pedagogic task, a 'scientific and ethical *education* of our nation' (to Carl von Gersdorff, 12 December).

1871

Growing reluctance to continue as a classical philologist. From February: on sick leave in the Swiss Alps.

1872

2 January: *The Birth of Tragedy from the Spirit of Music*. At first not a single German review of *The Birth of Tragedy* appears. Then a public censure by a Bonn colleague, H. Usener: 'Anyone who has written a thing like that is finished as a scholar.'

January-March: five public lectures, 'On the Future of our Educational Institutes' (published posthumously), delivered at Basle.

May: attends the laying of the foundation-stone of the Bayreuth theatre. Hans von Bülow, the conductor, finds no musical merit in Nietzsche's *Manfred Meditation*.

This is *the first* of the sixteen years of Nietzsche's creative life, *the last* in which he was to enjoy tolerable health.

1873

The first of *Thoughts out of Season* (an attack on the 1864 edition of D. F. Strauss's *Der alte und der neue Glaube* [*The New Faith and the Old*].

Wagner offended *and* pacified. Friendship with Paul Rée, writer on psychology.

Attacks of migraine, worsening eyesight.

1874

Thoughts out of Season: II 'On the Uses of History'; III 'Schopenhauer as Educator'.

The pattern of Nietzsche's life is now established: cures in spas, journeys in the Swiss Alps, university terms at Basle.

1875

Friendship with Peter Gast (i.e. Heinrich Köselitz), a young musician, who will write to Nietzsche's dictation and prepare his illegible manuscripts for the press.

'I practise unlearning *the haste of wanting-to-know* from which all scholars suffer . . . I shall not acquire health sooner than I really *deserve* it . . .' (to Gersdorff, 13 December).

'Spiritual crises' mounting.

1876

Thoughts out of Season: IV 'Richard Wagner in Bayreuth'.

Feeling of solitude increased by marriage of several friends. Sudden half-hearted proposal of marriage to a young Dutchwoman, Mathilde Trampedach.

From 15 October: one year sick-leave. Genoa, Naples, Sorrento.

Meets the Wagners at Sorrento. Wagner expounds the Christian motifs and symbolism of *Parsifal*. Nietzsche finds Wagner's Christian convictions 'mere playacting', a wholly expedient attempt 'to come to an arrangement with Germany's ruling powers, which have now turned pious'. The two men will never meet again.

1877

Sorrento, Ragaz.

'All that my very problematic thinking and writing have ever achieved was to make me very ill; as long as I was really a scholar, I was healthy!' (to Meysenbug, 1 July).

Reading Shelley's *Prometheus Unbound*: 'I bow deeply before one who can experience *this* within himself and is capable of bodying it forth' (to Rohde, 28 August).

'*I yearn for myself* – that has really been the continuous theme of my last ten years' (to Marie Baumgartner, 30 August).

1878

Human, All-Too-Human: a Book for Free Spirits. Philosophy in a new key, the key of 'becoming: there are no *eternal facts*, just as there are no absolute truths. Therefore what is needed from now on, is *historical philosophizing* and the virtue of being content with that.'

Complaint about 'the estrangement of so many friends and acquaintances' (to Gast, 31 May).

Basle household dissolved.

Letter of 15 July – Nietzsche describes himself as 'a philosopher of life'.

On 18 November he speaks of 'my shattered health'.

1879

Aphoristic supplement to *Human, All-Too-Human*.

'Solitary as I was . . . I now took sides against myself and for everything that would hurt me – me especially – and would come hard to me' (from the 1886 preface).

14 June: physical state deteriorating, resigns Chair.

Visits the Engadine for the first time.

'In the middle of life I am so "surrounded by death" that it may take me at any hour . . . A good drop of *oil* has been poured out through me, I know, and what I have done won't be forgotten' (to Gast, 11 September). 'The manuscript [of *Human* . . .] . . . is purchased so dearly and with so much hardship that nobody who had the choice would have written it at that price' (to Gast, 5 October).

1880

Concluding section of *Human: All-Too-Human*: II 'The Wanderer and his Shadow'.

Naumburg, Bolzano, Venice, Marienbad, Frankfurt, Heidelberg, Locarno, Stresa, winter in a freezing garret in Genoa.

1881

Aurora [or *The Dawn*]: *Thoughts on Moral Prejudices.*
'As for my attitude to Christianity . . . in my heart I have
   never really vilified it, and from my childhood days I
   frequently made a great inward effort towards its ideals,
   though in the last years I always came up against sheer
   impossibility' (to Overbeck, 23 June).
First stay in Sils Maria. Here, '6000 feet above man and
   time', there came to him what he later (in *Ecce Homo*,
   written 1888) called 'the fundamental conception [of
   Zarathustra], that is, the idea of the *Eternal Recurrence*
   . . .' Periods of depression, too: 'I think of myself as
   the scrawl which an unknown power scribbles across
   a sheet of paper, to try out *a new pen*' (to Gast, end of
   August).

1882

The Joyous [or *Gay*] *Science.*
'God is dead' pronounced for the first time.
Falls in love with a young Russian girl, Lou von Salomé
   – Nietzsche's only love-affair? Asks Paul Rée, himself
   in love with Lou, to propose to her on his behalf. Both
   are turned down.
His complete break with his friends; feels bitterly betrayed
   by Lou and Rée: 'What do my fantasies matter to you?
   Even my truths have not mattered to you. I should
   like you both to ponder that I am a headache-plagued
   half-lunatic, crazed by too much solitude' (to Lou and
   Rée, mid-December).
'If I can't discover the alchemists' trick of turning even
   this filth into gold, then I am lost' (to Overbeck,
   Christmas Day).

1883

Thus Spoke Zarathustra: a Book for All and None parts I and II. Nietzsche's own estimates swing from one extreme to another: '. . . behind all those simple and strange words lies my *deepest seriousness* and my *whole philosophy*' (to Gersdorff, 28 June), and 'Nothing can be made good any more, I shall make nothing good any more. Why make anything? Which reminds me of my latest foolishness – I mean my *Zarathustra*' (to Meysenbug, end of March).

13 February: Wagner dies. 'Wagner was by far the *fullest* man I have ever known . . .' (to Overbeck, 22 February). 'It was hard to be for six years the enemy of the man one most reveres . . .' (to Gast, 19 February).

Nietzsche's decision '*not* to live in Germany, and *not* to live with my relations' (to Overbeck, 27 October).

1884

Thus Spoke Zarathustra part III.

'I am now in all probability *the most independent man in Europe*. My goals and tasks reach wider than those of anyone else' (to Overbeck, before 2 May).

'I flatter myself that with this book I have brought the German language to its peak of perfection . . . My style is a *dance*, a playing with symmetries of all kinds and a leapfrogging and mockery of those symmetries . . .' (to Rohde, 22 February).

Having fallen out, because of Lou, with his sister, Nietzsche remains unreconciled.

1885

Thus Spoke Zarathustra part IV. Printed privately, with financial help from Gersdorff. 'I am forty years old and have never earned a single penny from my numerous books' (to Gersdorff, 12 February).

Nietzsche's letters become more and more fraught with tension.

1886

Beyond Good and Evil.

Buys back the copyright of his previous books from incompetent publisher Ernst Schmeitzner, and writes new introduction to them (except *Thoughts out of Season*). Describes the theme of *Beyond Good and Evil* as 'the contradiction between every conception of morality and every scientific [i.e. biological and physical] conception of *life*' (to Burckhardt, 22 September).

Growing feeling of solitude (to Overbeck, 5 August).

1887

Genealogy of Morals: 'Moral-historical studies . . . psychological problems of the most exacting kind – it almost requires more courage to pose them than to risk answering them' (to Burckhardt, 14 November).

'I have no respect left for present-day Germany, even though, hedgehog-fashion, the country is bristling with arms. It represents the most stupid, the most depraved, the most mendacious form of "the German spirit" that ever was' (to Seydlitz, 24 February).

Great praise for Wagner's *Parsifal* (to Gast, 21 January). Discovers French translation of two Dostoyevsky stories.

2 December: beginning of correspondence with Danish critic Georg Brandes, whom he praises for describing his, Nietzsche's, writings as *'aristocratic radicalism'*. Illuminating self-analysis: 'In the scale of my experiences, the rarer, more distant, thinner tonalities predominate over the normal middle ones ... I am suspicious of dialectics, even of reasons. More important, it seems to me, is courage ... I myself have only rarely the courage of what I know.'

The Will to Power. Since 1882 Nietzsche had been planning a systematic summation of his philosophy under this and several other headings. He wrote a number of outlines and tables of contents; perhaps the most viable of them is the one dated 17 March 1887; no definitive version was ever completed by him.

1888

The Wagner Case: a Musician's Problem; The Antichrist: a Curse upon Christianity; The Dionysos Dithyrambs; Twilight of the Idols (all published after his mental collapse).

Sojourns in Nice and Genoa. Afflicted by grave illnesses.

From 21 September to 9 January 1889 in Turin.

His sister Elisabeth's birthday letter to him causes him deep anguish: in it she asks whether he too is now 'beginning to be famous' even though nobody but 'a fine set of riff-raff, a few smart Jews included', believes in him.

Deussen visits Nietzsche in Sils-Maria (in September):

'Nietzsche seemed to drag himself along with difficulty . . . and his speech often became slurred, heavy and halting.'

Deussen and Meta von Salis help to cover Nietzsche's printing expenses. Nietzsche writes his letter of thanks 'in the midst of an infinitely difficult and decisive task which, *if it is understood*, will split the history of mankind in two. The meaning of it . . . is the *Revaluation of All Values*' (to Deussen, 14 September).

18 October: letter to Overbeck shows the first unmistakable signs of madness. Yet this letter also contains a brilliant interpretation of Germany's contribution to European civilization: '. . . this race now has "the Reich" on its mind, that recrudescence of petty states and cultural atomism, at the very moment when *the great question of values* is being asked for the first time'.

Process of breakdown gathers speed. Medical cause of the collapse is diagnosed as 'paralysis progressiva', i.e. 'tertiary paralysis', most probably syphilitic in origin. The scene of the catastrophe is Turin, where he feels blissfully happy: good music, excellent theatres, solicitous reverence from the waiters. But the bow snaps. The moment of affirmation has come at last, the 'yeasaying to life' has begun, *and nothing whatever happens*.

Proposes direct action: copies of *Ecce Homo* 'with a letter containing a declaration of war' are to go to Bismarck and the young Emperor William II (to Strindberg, 7 December).

1889

His very last letter (to Jakob Burckhardt, dated 6 January) begins: 'Dear Professor, in the end I would have much preferred being a Basle professor to being God. But I did not dare to carry my private egoism so far that for its sake I should omit the creation of the world . . .'; and it ends: 'I have had Caiaphas put in chains, last summer I too was being crucified by German doctors in a very wearisome way. William [the Second][1], Bismarck and all anti-Semites abolished . . .'

3 January: causes a public commotion in a square in Turin by throwing his arms round an old carthorse, and is carried to his lodgings.

Overbeck hastens to Turin, escorts Nietzsche first to Basle, then to Jena. First Nietzsche's mother, then his sister Elisabeth supervise the nursing of him. He lingers on for almost 12 years, gentle and childlike, incapable of coherent thought.

1900

Dies on 25 August.

Overbeck, in a memorandum, observes that 'To me it seems quite possible . . . that he did not bring madness into life with him, but that it was a product of his way of life . . . I could not entirely resist the thought that Nietzsche's illness was simulated – an impression derived from my long-standing experience of his habit of taking on many different masks.'

3 The Birth of Tragedy

Nietzsche's first work, *The Birth of Tragedy from the Spirit of Music* (1872), is the masterpiece of his classical apprenticeship. It exemplifies what Nietzsche means by an authentic use of scholarship, yet it is far from being the sort of enquiry that we describe as 'disinterested' or 'purely academic'. The book was violently attacked on its first publication, after which a lengthy and partly scurrilous polemic ensued; it permanently destroyed Nietzsche's credentials as a university teacher; and it is still regarded by some as a cuckoo in the nest of classical scholarship, the very pattern of works described as 'brilliant but unsound'. Why?

For one thing, its manner of exposition refutes the time-honoured distinction between creative and learned, 'wissenschaftlich' prose. Nietzsche convinces as much by anecdotes and extended metaphor as he does by discursive argument. Moreover, the hybrid character of the book becomes clear when we discover that it pursues not one but several distinct and highly ambitious aims. It is intended to give an account of and illuminate (rather than explain) the origins of the greatest tradition of Western literature, the art of classical tragedy, and the culture in which it flourished and died. It contains a major proposal to re-create, in contemporary Germany, those conditions which had made the arts of classical Greece possible and had led to the efflorescence of her uniquely rich culture. It is a philosophical undertaking in the sense of giving an extended description of what Nietzsche takes to be a dichotomy in the very depths of the human disposition.

And, finally, the book is 'a contribution to the science of aesthetics'. It is the first of all those sketches and reflections which, throughout the next sixteen years, will accompany Nietzsche's moral-existential thinking, sometimes merging with it, then again drawn up in conscious opposition to it – aspects of that enigma which never ceases to fascinate him: What is the function of the aesthetic in the world?

Like Schopenhauer before him, Nietzsche sees the fullest embodiment of the aesthetic in music. He follows scholarly tradition by placing the origin of tragedy in the chorus, though for him the important thing is not its message but its dithyrambs. He sees the chorus, quite literally, as the crowd of satyrs accompanying Dionysus, the god of the vine and of ecstasy, on his drunken revels through the forest. In their ecstasy and in the dirge they sing, the satyrs and their god are one: they are a single, undivided expression of the impermanence and desolation of human existence, its 'ground of experience'. This 'ground' is like the earth that was without form and like the darkness that was upon the face of the deep. It stands for and *is* a single, fundamental human disposition, involving as yet no division between self and world, and thus no knowledge that is not instinctive and intuitive.

This one-ness is broken as soon as men come to know, and to reflect upon, their ephemeral state. In the wake of the satyrs King Midas roams through the forest, seeking Silenus, Dionysus's companion and foster-father, who is hiding from him. At last the mortal King catches the elusive god and forces him to speak – to tell the most devastating of all truths: 'You want to know what life is about?' Silenus asks. 'The best is out of your reach, for the best of all things is not to have been born, not to be, to be nothing!' [*BT* § 3] Faced with this knowledge, men become self-conscious, sober, reflective, filled with tragic

apprehension. Now they make it their task to hide the
terrible knowledge of their ephemeral state from themselves and from those who watch their revels, and they
do this by turning their apprehension of the truth into
an ecstatic show, a drama. However, by 'drama' Nietzsche
means not an action but an episode or scene – even 'a
fundamental mood' – of great pathos [*CW* § 9]. Just as
many poets attest the origin of lyrical poems in a musical
mood, so (Nietzsche argues) the origin of this pathos is
in music. It connects drama with a non-verbal, chthonian
world which he considers more authentic than the world
of words and mere 'literature'. It is the essence of the
show which the chorus enacts that it should both preserve
the pathos of their new knowledge and make that knowledge bearable, and the god who helps them to fashion it
into a bearable – indeed a beautiful – form is the sun god
Apollo.

Art is not the trimmings of life [*BT* 1871 preface, dedi-
cated to Wagner], but a total re-enacting of it in another
medium. Its vitality and importance is confirmed by
Nietzsche's insistence on its psychosomatic parallel. As
Dionysus is the god of chaos, fruitfulness and *ecstasy*, so
Apollo is the god of ordered form and of the *dream* seen
as the silent re-casting of life. Tragedy is born at the
conjuncture of these two fundamental impulses, to which
Nietzsche gives the names of their tutelary deities, the
Dionysian and the Apolline. What the artist, its creator,
experiences is

> . . . the whole divine comedy of life, including the inferno
> . . . not like mere shadows on the wall – for he lives and
> suffers with these scenes – and yet not without that fleeting
> sensation of illusion. And perhaps many will, like myself,
> recall how amid the dangers and terrors of dreams they

have occasionally called out to themselves in self-encourage-
ment and not without success : 'It is a dream! I wish to
dream on!' [*BT* § 1]

The formulation is among the most accurate and beautiful in Nietzsche's work, but it is as precarious as the
moment it describes. The image-making faculty is not yet
contrasted with consciousness, or indeed self-conscious-
ness. The art thus characterized may not be the art of
classical Greek drama that Nietzsche is about to describe,
but it fits a work like Wagner's *Die Meistersinger* or
modern, post-Nietzschean drama to perfection. Appealing
to a common psychic experience – or, at least, to an
experience *he* considers common and which is certainly
not eccentric – Nietzsche draws from it the view that
drama is both dream and consciousness of dream. But this
positive evaluation of consciousness is not maintained.
The next step in the argument, in the later sections of
The Birth of Tragedy and then in the second of *Thoughts
out of Season*, will be the exaltation of a healthy, creative
life at the cost of a merely intellectual knowledge of the
world, followed by Nietzsche's strange paeans to the unconscious, 'the natural' and 'the instinctive' as authentic
modes of experience. (We cannot blame Nietzsche for the
ghastly company in which this enthusiasm for authenticity
in its various forms will land him in our time, when he
can no longer 'prevent people from doing mischief with
me' [*EH* IV § 10]. Yet we must marvel at the paradox,
for which we have lost the taste, whereby this most intellectual and conscious of modern thinkers invokes values
to which he is himself a stranger.)

But to return to *The Birth of Tragedy*: the aim of
Nietzsche's dialectic, then, is to maintain the interplay
between two fundamental modes of knowledge-and-life

which encompass his view of tragedy: its Dionysian foundation and the Apolline order imposed upon it. The argument has its roots in Schopenhauer's dichotomy of the World as Will and the World as Idea; it is related to Aristotle's distinction of matter and form; its chief ancestor is Schiller's dichotomy of the 'naïve' and the 'sentimental' modes of poetry. It belongs among the three or four truly memorable arguments in the history of aesthetics. Its epitome is mastered energy, its poles are chaos and epic harmony. When the Dionysian element rules, ecstasy and inchoateness threaten; when the Apolline predominates, the tragic feeling recedes. Of the two, the Dionysian remains the fundamental, but the balance in the great works of tragic art is subtle and easily upset. Changes in this balance provide Nietzsche with the data of a rudimentary literary history. The balance is achieved for the first time in Aeschylus, and then again in Sophocles; by the time Euripides comes to dominate the literary scene, the Dionysian element is attenuated and at last all but completely suppressed, and in Euripides's *The Bacchae* the thwarted god takes his revenge.

The predominance of the Dionysian element in the masterpieces of Greek tragedy implies, first, that for Nietzsche intuition and ecstasy are the only authentic modes of artistic creation. It implies, secondly, an interest in the origins and genealogy rather than in the structure of a work of art – it is axiomatic for Nietzsche that the origins of a work of art wholly determine its value. And the dominance of Dionysus assumes, finally, an unreflective belief on the part of the playwrights' public in the germinal episodes or myths from which tragedy is fashioned, a belief which the poets share with their public. What these myths represent is not the mimesis of a plot (not, as in the famous opening sentence of Aristotle's

Poetics, 'the imitation of an *action*'), but the articulation of *a fundamental mood*, or what we would call a style of life. Throughout Nietzsche's aesthetic writings it is this conception of a mood or style of life which is his main concern. This 'Lebensgefühl' is, for him, more fundamental than rational argument, because it is its source.

The decline of Greek tragedy begins where creative ecstasy is suppressed and has to give way to cold calculation. Now the old myths cease to be experienced as parts of an ecstatic religious ritual and become objects of rational analysis, the gods and their stories come to be judged according to the prosy maxims of reasoned justice. By a characteristic turn of Nietzsche's philosophical imagination this history of Greek tragedy emerges as a paradigm for every other cultural development, including the decline into decadence and degeneration he sees taking place around him.

Nietzsche's choice of a biological metaphor is revealing. Art is one of the ruses of life, tragedy (we recall) has always had a vital function: to protect men from a full knowledge of the life-destroying doom that surrounds them, and at the same time to refresh their zest for life from tragedy's own dark Stygian sources. The degeneration of tragedy at the hands of Euripides and of Socrates (whom Nietzsche here presents as ugly and artistically ungifted) means that it can no longer fulfil its vital function. The new literary forms – Platonic dialogue and Aesopean fable – are effete parodies which in their superficiality and optimism no longer acknowledge the reality of the abyss of suffering. Through these forms that instinctive feeling of awe and apprehension has been jeopardized – that feeling without which the life-blood of every culture runs into the sand. For true culture (Nietzsche argues) is only possible within that narrow boundary where knowledge is manageable yet all that threatens life is not trivialized: an area bounded by a 'not yet' and a 'no longer'. The 'not yet', pure want, is the stage where the Dionysian song dominates to the extent of making articulation and individuation impossible (articulation of inchoate responses till they become myth, and individuation of responses till they become individual characters who enact the myth). And the 'no longer' is the prosy stage of rationalism, when the myths are accounted for in discursive and abstract terms; explained in rational-causal terms; and thus explained away.

What are the conditions under which that narrow space between 'not yet' and 'no longer' comes into being? Can it be deliberately created? When, in the last sections of *The Birth of Tragedy*, Nietzsche writes his great panegyric of Richard Wagner as the man who will 're-create' the cultic and mythical situation of Sophoclean tragedy, the deeply problematic nature of his undertaking becomes clear. Nietzsche's is not a narrowly 'aesthetic' view but a cultic vision, encompassing the whole life of a nation, and what he is seeking is no less than a concrete objective correlative to this vision in the world around him. He finds it – or he thinks he finds it – in Richard Wagner, the most richly gifted of his contemporaries. He is anxious to attribute to Wagner's art that same cultic quality which he – Nietzsche – saw in the great tragedians of Greece. Wagner readily agrees. The break comes, *not* because Wagner repudiates the role of modern mystagogue, but because (in Nietzsche's view) he cynically exploits it.

There are battles which are lost. Who could fail to sympathize with Nietzsche when he invokes 'the rebirth of a German myth', or when he writes, 'Without a myth every culture loses its healthy, creative natural power. Only a horizon enclosed by myths gives unity to a whole cultural movement' [§ 23]? Yet the fact that Nietzsche's critical observation is no less relevant to the condition of our culture than it was to his, does not make his plea for the birth of a new myth less pre-posterous. The vital need of the age (he is saying) is for a new kind of innocence, an archaic state of cult and culture, for a sophisticated breakthrough into unsophistication. We for our part have learned that studied instinctiveness is humbug, and that whatever is wrong with our culture, it is not excess of consciousness.

The Birth of Tragedy contains the epitome of Nietzsche's aesthetics: his acceptance of Schopenhauer's ideas on music and his re-valuation of Schopenhauer's idea of the will in the world; his challenge to the (originally Kantian) idea of aesthetics as a 'disinterested' and therefore (in Nietzsche's view) defective mode of life; his contempt for language as an inferior medium, inadequate to the task of conveying the deepest mystery of life; and, following from that, Nietzsche's ironical repudiation of Socratic – dialectical – reasoning and what he regards as its eudae-monic, optimistic shallowness. And it is here that Nietzsche expresses for the first time those two maxims which will encompass his aesthetic thinking to the end.

The first [§ 7] represents a reversal of the Schopenhauer-ian scheme which is more radical than Nietzsche as yet knows: If man is to be saved from the renunciation of his will and from the terrible nihilism to which he is driven by the awareness of his condition, then 'it is art that saves him, and through art' – for its own purpose – 'life'. The second maxim is repeated three times [§§ 5, 24 and 1886 preface], yet for all that remains disconnected from the main argument of the book:

4 Historical Philosophizing

I

Nietzsche begins his philosophical venture by taking issue with the cultural situation of the German Empire of 1871. Among the components of that curious amalgam of romantic medievalism and Prussian efficiency known as the Second Reich is a strong patriotic concern with the past, supported by a powerful tradition of historical research. When, in the second of his *Thoughts out of Season* (1874), Nietzsche enquires into 'The Use and Disadvantage of History for Life', the very title of his essay questions one of the cultural axioms of the day – that a knowledge of its own past necessarily strengthens the life of a given society. Yet his thoughts are less 'out of season' than he seems to think. The bulk of his argument is designed to show how the historical consciousness may succeed in its patriotic aim and why it so often fails to achieve it. He has no fear that historical scholarship will be corrupted by what in effect are political ends. Since he makes no distinction between the needs of individual men, of societies and of states, he does not acknowledge 'the historical spirit' as a political factor at all, but sees it as an aspect of the culture of individual men. They alone count. A people or a state is no more than 'the masses' [*TS* II § 9] led by a few great men.

The enhancement of man as a species is the end purpose of mankind [§ 9]. Whatever will improve the vitality and passion for life of great men is to be commended as the right kind of historical science. Academic history's aspirations to comprehensiveness, its preoccupation with endless factual details and its ideal of impartial objectivity are

49

bound to be in conflict with 'the needs of great men'. Truth is not objectivity but the will to justice [§ 6], and historical justice, which is bound to be relative to the character of the historian, is the business of judging the past in respect of its contribution to human greatness. 'History is endured only by strong personalities – the weak ones are extinguished by it. [§ 5.]

History at its most life-enhancing is seen, in a Churchillian manner, as the story of great men with heroic ideals and a monumental capacity for self-sacrifice in the service of those ideals. Nietzsche presents such men not merely as examples to those who come after them but, more interestingly, as the creators of a spiritual and intellectual atmosphere [§ 7], of *the human horizon* that is appropriate to a given society [§ 1]. This horizon is made up of men's vital beliefs and ideas, and of the myths in which these beliefs and ideas are enshrined; if this horizon, this 'atmosphere' is destroyed or damaged, most men are condemned to sterility, mediocrity and death (and mediocrity, for Nietzsche, is a sort of death). Here, as so often, Nietzsche's cultural criticism impinges on our ecological thinking: we may think of his metaphor as analogous to the ionosphere which surrounds the earth and which, if it is damaged or modified, is bound to affect our life in all its aspects. There is no doubt that Nietzsche at all times saw the power of ideas as equal to that of physical forces, and often as continuous with those forces. Hence our metaphor from modern ecology is not as anachronistic as it may seem: like the greatest of the German Romantic poets, Hölderlin and Novalis, Nietzsche sees the destruction of the physical horizon as directly consequent on the break-up of a system of religious or philosophical ideas.

Two kinds of ideas threaten or destroy 'the human

atmosphere': one kind because it is accepted as true, the other because it is shown to be untrue. Among the former is a decadent society's preoccupation with its heroic past (the idea of past grandeur dwarfing the present and threatening to extinguish the future is likely to strike us as familiar).

But what happens to 'life' when the picture of a heroic past is shown to be untrue? The past then turns out to be the thoroughly unheroic product of the spirit of vengeance and grudgingness. Human history, permeated by this spirit, is seen to be little more than a series of reactions by the weak and 'underprivileged' who, in a variety of ignoble ways, resist and revenge themselves on those naturally endowed with nobility and strength of purpose – they take revenge by creating a scale of values (or rather 'anti-values') of their own, a morality of their own, which they then impose by means of blackmail on the gods' own aristocrats of body and soul. What happens to the enchantment of 'life' when we discover that *this* is the origin of *all* morality, and that the idea of conscience too (which is the instrument of blackmail) is the product of the spirit of resentment and grudging envy? Can men endure the discovery that their metaphysical and religious beliefs are fictitious, are no more than *part of their human horizon*? Is anything left of the splendours of human history except a tragical-comical spectacle for non-existent gods? The destructive conclusion is at hand that to recognize history for a fiction and a fiction for what it is, a lie, is to deprive history of its 'usefulness for life'.

Some of these questions take us beyond 'The Use and Disadvantage of History', yet it is proper to mention them here because they are extrapolations of two fundamental questions which are considered in this early essay: Is life possible without the consolations and protection of a belief in God, once that belief has been shown to be part of a myth [§ 8]? And, more generally: Is there knowledge which should not be pursued because it is noxious to 'life', and is it possible to devise rules – 'a doctrine of the hygiene of life' [§ 10] – whereby to set limits to the pursuit of such knowledge? These are among the questions which will occupy Nietzsche throughout his conscious life.

II

At the beginning of his next work, *Human, All-Too-Human* (1878), Nietzsche writes, in a spirit of criticism which reminds us of Marx:

> Lack of historical sense is the hereditary defect of all philosophers . . . Many of them take man automatically as he has most recently been shaped by the impression of a particular religion or even of particular political events . . . But everything [that is] has become [what it is]; there are neither eternal facts nor indeed eternal verities. Therefore what is needed from now on is historical philosophizing, and with it the virtue of modesty.

And in a note written at the same time:

> What separates us from Kant, as from Plato and Leibnitz, is that we believe only in Becoming – in intellectual matters too; we are *historical* through and through . . . The way Heraclitus and Empedocles thought is alive once more. [*Mus* XVI p. 9]

'Historical philosophizing', then, is one of Nietzsche's two principal methods of examining the beliefs and ideas of a given society, which to him are always primarily the beliefs and ideas of its great men. (The other is the 'psychological method', the method of 'my evil eye', which looks for the hidden motives.) In this respect Nietzsche knows himself and his age to be deeply influenced by the historicizing thought of Hegel (even though he rejects the notion that world history reached its culminating point when he – Hegel – got the Chair of Philosophy in Berlin [*TS* II § 8.]) But what is this 'historical philosophizing'? My example of the way Nietzsche applies his method to a major philosophical topic comes from *The Twilight of the Idols* (1888), where Nietzsche is at his most intellectually vigorous.

In a sketch entitled
    'How the "True World" Finally Became a Fable'
and subtitled 'The History of an Error', he presents the history of Platonism in six stages [*TI* III]:

> (1) The true world, attainable for the sage, the pious, the virtuous man – he lives in it, *he is it*. (This is the oldest form of the idea, relatively clever, simple, convincing. It is the paraphrase of the proposition, 'I, Plato, *am* the truth.')

At this first stage, the 'true' or metaphysical world is identical with the world in which men live: not all or any men, though, but only the elect. (The feeling of cosmic oneness – 'he is it' – is also a moral quality.) By saying that the virtuous man *is* that world, and that Plato *is* the truth, Nietzsche wants not only to stress the personal nature of truth, but also to portray (as Hölderlin had done) an age whose religious 'ideals' are not remote and 'transcendent', but inherent in men's world. The 'true world' is not a 'Platonic' idea, it has *not yet* been alienated into the object of a metaphysical doctrine: it is Plato's world, not the world of Platonism.

(2) The true world, now unattainable, but promised to the sage, the pious, the virtuous man ('the sinner who repents'). (Progress of the idea: it becomes subtler, more enticing, less graspable – *it becomes female*, it becomes Christian.)

At this stage, true being or reality has been pushed out of this world, to the very edge that men can reach. The sensible world is no longer the meaningful world – meaning is 'beyond'. This new situation makes for a correspondingly finer, 'subtler' awareness of the impalpable and the merely promised, but it also places the idea of the 'true world' as the repository of all stable values in a remote and erotically enticing perspective. This displacement Nietzsche (like Hölderlin before him) identifies with the advent of Christianity, and among its consequences he sees the emergence of a new morality. It is a morality, not of the old aristocratic kind whose devices were 'good' and 'bad', but the new, religiously sanctioned, slavish morality of 'good and evil'. The point of making 'the idea' change sex seems merely gratuitous, a piece of bad taste. Yet it is significant of the way in which, for Nietzsche, the philosophical argument is accompanied by a physiological one, the abstract by the concrete. These stylistic incarnations are often embarrassing. The ensuing embarrassment, however, heightens one's perception: we recognize them as Nietzsche's attempts to give life to his reflection and to rebut the body/soul dualism.

(3) The true world, unattainable, unprovable, unpromisable, but the mere thought of it is a consolation, an obligation, an imperative. (Basically this is the old sun again, but seen through mist and scepticism; the idea has become sublime, pale, northern, Königsbergian.)

'The mere thought of it': in this account of the Kantian

('Königsbergian') re-interpretation of Platonism, the 'true world' is even further removed from the world of the senses. Since it is that in which the world and all thought is grounded (and therefore not the object of thought), 'the idea' offers 'consolation' for the absence of truth and stability from the sensible world. It offers 'an obligation' to obey the commands which 'the mere thought' of transcendence imposes upon men; and it offers 'an imperative', i.e. the moral law which Kant had conceived as a postulate of practical reason and thus as the only exception to the rule that reason can never reflect upon its own transcendent foundations. The world depicted in this third stage is the cold and bleak Protestant world, which Heinrich Heine had guyed in his funny stories about the choleric Martin Luther and the cold comforts of the Reformation. The dominant mode of this world is abstractness, in which Nietzsche sees the fountain-head of modern science.

> (4) The true world – unattainable? at any rate unattained. And, being unattained, it is also *unknown*. Therefore *not* consoling, redeeming, obligating: for what obligation could something unknown impose on us? (Grey morning. Reason's first yawning, the cock-crow of positivism.)

We are now moving closer to Nietzsche's own age, the post-Kantian nineteenth century which no longer accepts – should no longer accept – the consolations of religious metaphysics. More than once Nietzsche has 'unmasked' German Idealism as a substitute-religion. (In *Ecce Homo* XIV § 3, he will write: 'On the roll of knowledge the Germans are inscribed with nothing but dubious names, *all* that they have ever produced have been "unconscious" coiners – an appellation as appropriate to Fichte, Schelling,

Schopenhauer, Hegel, Schleiermacher as it is to Leibnitz and Kant: they are *all* merely Schleiermacher . . .' i.e. 'makers of veils', obfuscators.)

It seems that Nietzsche welcomes this new age with its lack of illusion and the first stirrings of an energetic, self-contained rationality: is it not braver, rougher but also more honest than the effeminate eighteenth century, the age of transcendentally cushioned rationalism [*WKG* VIII/ 2 pp. 104f]? Yet there is nothing enthusiastic about the image with which the description of this stage closes.

> (5) The 'true' world – now an idea that is no use for anything and does not even provide the grounds of an obligation – an idea that has become useless and redundant and *therefore* a refuted idea: let us abolish it! (Bright day; breakfast; return of *bon sens* and cheerfulness; Plato blushing embarrassedly; pandemonium of all free spirits.)

Is this a picture of Nietzsche's own age or of the future? The cobwebs of all transcendentalisms have been cleared away, men may now rely on the testimony of their senses only, reason's battle has been fought and won; so complete was the victory that no rancour or resentment, no aggressiveness remain. The historicized idea is now superseded by that stage of 'cheerfulness' – or is it 'serenity'? the German term, 'Heiterkeit', means either – which in Nietzsche's later works figures increasingly as the dominant virtue with which to oppose the honourable but cheerless 'spirit of gravity'. But if this reflection is what it claims to be – a realistic account of Nietzsche's own age, or at least of the future with its roots in his age – why not stop there and then? Why do 'all the free spirits' make a devilish noise? Has the historicized idea not been fully refuted after all?

(6) We have abolished the true world: what world has remained? the world of appearances perhaps? ... But no! with the true world we have also abolished the world of appearances! (Noon; moment of the briefest shadow, end of the largest error; the zenith of humanity; INCIPIT ZARATHUSTRA.)

Nietzsche no longer writes 'We have abolished the "true" world.' The refutation of the Platonic idea is to be followed by a collapse of the entire terminology of religious and metaphysical dualisms: there is to be neither appearance nor a reality postulated in opposition to appearance (just as in *Beyond Good and Evil*, 1886, he sets out to refute that notion of 'good' which had arisen in opposition to 'evil'). At this highest point in the history of man, when the antithesis between the sensuous and the suprasensuous too has been abolished, enters Zarathustra; and with him comes the reign of the Superman, whose love of the Earth will validate all.

Or will it? A terrible ambiguity clings to the formulation of that final stage. 'Incipit Zarathustra' echoes 'Incipit tragoedia' – the opening sentence of the last section of the fourth (and provisionally the last) book of *The Joyous Science* (1882), which in turn is repeated verbatim as the opening section of *Thus Spoke Zarathustra* (1883). The 'tragedy' that now begins tells of Zarathustra's self-sacrifice and descent among the ranks of men ('human, all-too-human the best of them') and, by implication ('When Zarathustra was thirty years old . . .'), of Christ's self-sacrificial descent. If, with that echo in mind, we now think once more about the sentence with which the sketch of the last stage opened – 'We have abolished the true world: what world has remained?' – we see its meaning radically altered. What it expresses is no longer the joy of intellectual and therefore existential liberation, but a feeling of deprivation and loss; the high noon becomes the moment when the sun's merciless rays pierce every darkness, every nook and corner of ancient pieties and divine comfort; and Zarathustra, serene teacher of the doctrine of the Superman, becomes the prophet of doom.

The two meanings of the last stage do not cancel each other out, they are locked in an ambiguity which remains unresolved. What is to be the future and the fate of mankind? The serene life of spirits who are freed from ancient illusions and false comforts, or a world empty of all purpose and meaning, the reign of Nihilism everlasting? Freed from metaphysics, will the world be more joyful? Or was 'the resentment of the metaphysicians against the real' a *creative* act [*WP* § 579], so that metaphysics became a source of 'reality' after all; and has man, in destroying metaphysics, destroyed his own horizon and his own world? Or does the issue depend on what *you* are, on whether 'you become what you are'? Human authenticity, expressed in the 'will to power', moves into the centre of Nietzsche's argument.

5 Three Moral Experiments

What kind of philosopher is Nietzsche? His philosophical consciousness never comes to rest, is never reconciled to the restrictions of any one method, any one mode of enquiry, yet a discernible unity of some kind informs his philosophizing.[1] There is no system, yet there is a very distinct style of thinking.

Anyone who has read even a few pages of Nietzsche's writings will note that the arguments on the page give rise to a curious double feeling, a sort of *changeant* effect. An awareness of that exhilarating intellectual energy which I have mentioned – Nietzsche's determination to think beyond accepted opinions and conventional divisions across 'subjects' and 'disciplines' – goes hand in hand with an embarrassment which occasionally borders on irritation. An obvious source of this irritation seem to be Nietzsche's notorious opinions on certain topics – such as war, race, nationality, women – on which, for good reasons and bad, we are touchy. But we soon discover that the source of our feeling is more general. It is his inability to mention anything – any fact, observation, guess, suspicion or hypothesis – without almost immediately capping it with a value judgement. Value judgements – assent or condemnation; *yes* or *no* – are a constant mode of Nietzsche's thinking. And all of them – even those which are intended as part of a 'purely aesthetic' world and which he calls 'moralinfrei', as though morality were some kind of Aspirin or Veganin without which some people find life unendurable – all these judgements *slither into* moral ones. Inevitably, it seems, and often against his own intention, 'good or bad?' becomes 'good or evil?'.

We may place the various moral experiments which are conducted in his writings under three headings, for each of which *Hamlet* provides an appropriate motto:

(I) The problem of morality *versus* life: recalling Hamlet's remark to Rosencrantz, 'for there is nothing, either good or bad, but thinking makes it so.'

(II) The morality of the 'will to power': recalling Polonius's advice, 'This above all: to thine own self be true.'

(III) The morality of strenuousness: recalling Hamlet's gibe to Ophelia, 'This was sometime a paradox, but now the time gives it proof.'

This is not Nietzsche's own arrangement, nor is there a strict chronological sequence to these experiments, except that the first is mainly associated with the early, 'positivist' phase (up to *Joyous Science* of 1882), and the second is confined to the last four years. Only the second bears a label of Nietzsche's own devising, only 'the will to power' was ever intended by him as a systematic description and norm of human conduct.

I Morality *versus* Life

There can be no 'purpose' in history (he writes in the second of those *Thoughts out of Season* which was considered in the previous chapter): at any rate, there can be no true purpose which the mere passage of time could accomplish, and no (Hegelian) notion of inevitable progress either. History has no other function than to provide occasions for the generation of greatness, for 'The goal of humanity cannot lie at the end [of time], but only in its highest specimens.' [TS II § 9] Again, the Superman – the utopian project of *Thus Spoke Zarathustra* – is created as an expression of Nietzsche's concern with 'the whole man', whose enemy is fragmentation of knowledge and petrifaction of experience.[2] And the elaboration, in his last notes some fourteen years later, of a 're-valuation of all values' in the light of a ubiquitous 'will to power' is still in the service of the same idea: '. . . To what extent does a sacrifice of freedom, and even enslavement, provide the basis for a higher type [of man] . . . How may the development of mankind be sacrificed in order to help a species higher than man to come into being?' [*WP* § 859] This is not an ideal we contemplate with much sympathy. To return to our earlier comparison with Marx: we are not even sure which to think of as the greater evil: to be haunted by the spectre of injustice (a product of the inequality of the past) or by that of mediocrity (a product of our egalitarian present). Nietzsche has no doubt: his insistence that only the generation of greatness matters is indeed 'the most crucial point of his philosophy of history and theory of values – no less than the clue to his "aristocratic" ethics and his opposition to socialism and democracy'[3].

To this 'elevation of man' everything is a means and everything must be sacrificed. His view of men's past (that is, of their great 'historic' moments, to one side of any merely chronological development); of their present state, conduct and beliefs (in the age of European decadence and at the point of its merging into a destructive but liberating nihilism); and of their future hopes (seen in terms of a bio-psychological notion of breeding) – all these views are offered, not merely as descriptions of the human condition, but as parts of an all-encompassing pedagogic purpose.

This statement of Nietzsche's moral, or rather existential, project raises some obvious questions. What kind of 'improvement' and 'elevation of man' has he in mind?

What is his idea of nobility? What are the new values and the revaluation that is to lead to them? Evidently he is not another 'idealist philosopher' who puts his faith in 'the good will' or 'love' or 'compassion', or indeed in any one single and absolute state of mind. Not only are his arguments anti-idealist in tenor, but his insistence on a positive, creative morality grounded in 'the will to power' (itself more than a state of mind) is a direct challenge to the 'mind-matter' dichotomy on which every idealism is based. This new morality must not be abstract – more than that: it cannot be generalized, for generalization itself, the leveller of all distinction and excellence, is its enemy. Its material substance – that is, its concern with power – must not be at odds with its spiritual content, nor are the new moral values to be at odds with the biological values by which the healthy and strong part of mankind lives and should govern the rest; and Nietzsche does not hesitate to push the argument to the point where conventional morality – seen bluntly as the protective device of the 'underprivileged' in body and soul – is simply stood on its head, so that right (moral, legal as well as biological right) should be at one with might.

However, it can hardly be denied that this entire argument is erected on a scant foundation of material facts. The ethnological, historical and sociological views on which Nietzsche bases his moral observations are mostly derived from random collections of data, chance impressions, snippets of information; and the biological knowledge on which he bases his notions of breeding, which are later revised, is rudimentary and seems amateurish, it hardly goes beyond the Darwinian tags current at the time. But this amateurishness does not prevent him from accompanying all statements with value judgements: 'In order to live, one must evaluate.' [*WKG* VII/2 p. 179]

Of course there is no reason for thinking that one must be a competent historian, sociologist or biologist in order to philosophize about the moral nature of man. But equally one may ask why Nietzsche (e.g. in *Beyond Good and Evil*) should go out of his way to make detailed but doubtfully reliable observations about, say, 1789, or the utilitarian philosophy of Gower Street, the mentality of the French intelligentsia, the inherited character traits of command and obedience; why he should lean so heavily on notoriously vague words like 'instinct' and 'intuition', and concern himself with a hundred other miscellaneous subjects. To which the brief answer is : because Nietzsche does not want to be an 'idealist' philosopher. Not wanting to argue about such artificial moral conundrums as the undeserved sufferings of the just man or the consequences of pinching a spoonful of jam, he is forever in search of concrete facts and scientific data to serve as illustrations of a theory which rejects generality as inauthentic. Because the 'ideal' of nobility is to be *realized*, his moral philosophy moves between the devil of recalcitrant facts and the deep sea of an all-encompassing cosmology. He wants to be a practical philosopher (hence his great admiration for Emerson), yet he rebels against the tyranny of empiricism and 'our dubious taste for facts'.

We cannot be sure that Nietzsche is aware of his dilemma. For example, in *Beyond Good and Evil*, after a couple of pages of superior journalistic gossip [§ 251] about German policy on Jewish immigration and the desirability of marrying blue-blooded Junkers to clever Jewish girls, he stops in mid-sentence (not, we feel, a moment too soon) to apologize for indulging in this sort of chit-chat: 'to think about things that do not concern me [is] a first sign of being infected by the political disease.' But how can one discuss political problems without at least a touch of 'the political infection'? How can one consider, e.g. 'the European problem of breeding a new ruling class', even as a philosophical problem, with no more than a few ethnic anecdotes and observations and a few racial clichés to fall back on? Despising idealist utopias, he is forever searching for objective correlatives of his proposed re-valuation, and is forever dissatisfied with what he finds. As we shall see, the analogy with his linguistic views provides the pattern: in his philosophy, a thousand diverse utterances make little sense unless they are related to a silent cosmos of authentic being, a thousand diverse facts make little sense unless they are seen against some supreme – and ultimately unstable – notion of moral nobility. This is the 'pathos of distance' by which his philosophy is afflicted, *and from which it takes its sustenance*. To invoke this pathos on Nietzsche's behalf is to offer no excuse for his world-historical *obiter dicta*, doubtful biology, or his crudities about 'the English', 'the Germans' or 'the French'. But it does explain how he succeeds in arraying his few facts in a perspective that looks at first idiosyncratic yet turns out to convey an extraordinarily accurate picture – more often a forecast – of an actual ethnic or historical or cultural situation; how he comes to write such reflections as the sketch of 'the higher man' [§ 262], which must surely be among the most brilliant anticipations of twentieth-century intellectual fauna we know:

At these turning-points of history there often occurs the phenomenon of a splendid, luxuriant, jungle-like upward growth and burgeoning side by side and often interlocked and entwined – a kind of tropical acceleration and competing growth, monstrously wasteful and self-destructive, caused by the diverse egoisms – all turning on each other and as though exploding, all fighting each other 'for sun and air' and no longer able to derive any limit, any restraint, any forbearance from accepted morality. It was this morality itself that had stored up such enormous energy, and bent the bow in such a menacing way: – now it is spent, now it is becoming 'outlived'. Things have reached the dangerous and eerie point at which the greater, more complex, more comprehensive life *lives beyond* the old morality; the individual is forced to make his own laws, his own arts and stratagems of self-preservation, self-enhancement, self-redemption. Nothing but new whys and wherewithals; no more common formulas, incomprehension allied with contempt; decay, corruption and the highest desires horribly entangled; the genius of the race overflowing from every cornucopia of good and bad; an ill-omened coincidence of spring and autumn, full of new charms and veils characteristic of youthful corruption still unexhausted and untiring. Here once more there is danger, the mother of morality – great danger, only this time it resides in the individual, in neighbour and friend, in the street, in one's own child, one's own heart, in the most personal and intimate corner of every wish and will: what can the moralists of this new age preach? They discover, these acute observers and street-corner idlers, that the end is at hand, that everything about them is corrupt and corrupting, that nothing can last beyond the day after tomorrow, *one* species of man excepted, the incurably *mediocre*. The mediocre alone have the chance of continuing and of propagating themselves – they are the men of the future, the sole survivors; 'be like them! become mediocre!' is henceforth the only morality that still has any meaning or finds ears to hear it. But it is difficult to preach, this morality of mediocrity! for it can never admit what it is and what it wants! it must speak of moderation and dignity and duty and brotherly love – it will have a hard task to conceal its irony!

This, I would suggest, is the substance and style of

65

social insight and pre-vision on the grand scale. Its condition is déracinement – the pathos of distance, of not being very securely at home in the common world of men. In this respect Nietzsche's position is strikingly similar to that of Heine, whom he greatly admired, and to that of the Jews generally, with whom he occasionally identified: it is a compound of familiarity and critical detachment, of acceptance and 'the freedom that distance gives'. It is purchased at great cost to himself: 'I no longer have any idea at all which of my views bring comfort to people and which are hurtful to them,' he writes in 1881.[4] From this distance he sets up his man-traps and sleights of hand, and achieves his remarkable anticipations.

Nietzsche does not want to be an 'idealist' philosopher. Nothing is so characteristic of his way of thinking as his lack of interest in the classical problems of epistemology and his habit of converting every epistemological problem into a moral and existential one. The Kantian question, 'What can I reliably know?' is replaced by 'What is it good for me to know? What kind of knowledge is likely to further my will and being, and what kind will harm them? What is *my* good?'

The idealist ethic of knowledge, taken over by our scientists, is to be reversed. It is not man that is to be the servant of truth and knowledge (Nietzsche argues), but truth and knowledge shall be the servants of man. It is not knowledge and the pursuit of it that are absolute, but 'life' and the personal being of those who heed its demands. Knowledge is fashioned by man and corrupted by man, and therefore it is perfectly conceivable – this is a situation Nietzsche delights in conceiving – that one kind of person is entitled to one kind of knowledge but not to another. What is this entitlement? What is it that makes one person and not another, or one nation, or one age, entitled to metaphysical knowledge? Why is the question about the end-purpose of life appropriate to one culture and the undoing of another?

There is, ultimately, only one answer to these questions: the will to knowledge is to be identical with the will to power, which constitutes the being of man. The amount of knowledge any man is to acquire should be commensurate with a man's, or a nation's, strength of will and capacity for life: 'Once and for all, there are many things I do *not* wish to know. Wisdom sets a limit to knowledge, too.' [*TI* I § 5] The pursuit of knowledge is to be determined not by what *can* be known and what speculation, experiment and observation can make available (which provides very nearly *our* criteria for the pursuit of knowledge), but by a 'doctrine of the hygiene of life' [*TS* II § 10] – the idea of a personal entitlement to knowledge. It is an inegalitarian and unscientific idea (in the sense that, from Plato's *Meno* onwards, all scientific as opposed to esoteric knowledge is seen as available to all rational men), but it is not eccentric. As against scientific objectivity and the establishing of morally neutral 'laws', Nietzsche invokes the unity of the cognitive and moral aspects of man. Like Goethe before him he would like the quality of a man's knowledge (and, incidentally, also of his art) to depend on the quality of his moral-existential being, and (again like Goethe) Nietzsche hopes to achieve this without invoking a religious sanction. Yet the only analogy to this kind of reasoning is Christ's claim that the Pharisees' knowledge of the law is not enough and that only a certain moral state entitles to insight and judgement ('He that is without sin among you, let him first cast a stone at her,' *Joh*. 8/7). The moral problem posed by this injunction is surely insoluble without a religious sanction (it is because he invokes divine authority – *Joh*.

'8/15-17 – that Christ claims the right to denounce the Pharisees' legalism), and the same is true of Nietzsche's argument. Only by endowing 'life' with a quasi-religious, transcendent quality, and only by making man into a god, can he set up man as the measure of all things and all knowledge – yet Nietzsche's avowed aim is to do without all gods and all transcending of the human lot. And here we recognize the recurring pattern: the compulsion, repeated in one field of experience after another, that makes him group his reflections round an empty space – the space reserved for a grace from on high in a world where there is no grace and no on high either.

Yet if Nietzsche's attempts at rationalizing the idea of a personal entitlement to knowledge miscarry, his demonstration of what happens in the absence of such a 'doctrine of the hygiene of life' should not be lost on us. In a prophetic manner he describes the kind of freak whose knowledge is in excess of his existential capacity. In *Zarathustra* Nietzsche speaks of the papery imagination of intellectuals generally and historians in particular, who wield vast resources of information which in no way correspond to what they are as human beings.

The possibility of an unlimited pursuit of knowledge, heedless of consequences, is 'unmasked' as the symptom of an age of decadence, and of a life whose defences against its enemies have been undermined. Modern scientists live an unnerving existence in which their knowledge is in no sort of harmony with their world or their personal being [*GM* III § 23]; in a later note he adds: 'The fact that science as we today practise it is possible, proves that the elementary instincts which protect life have ceased to function . . .' [*WKG* VIII/3 pp. 18of] And here Nietzsche is uncovering a set of problems which, buried under the dogma of the absolute value of knowledge, are a good deal more urgent in our age than they were in his own. Of course, with the experience of fascist anti-intellectualism in our minds, we are bound to regard the idea of differing entitlements to knowledge as shockingly undemocratic: we feel the need to insist on a just and equitable distribution of knowledge as of everything. I do not propose to defend – though I shall try to explain – Nietzsche's lack of interest in this and all other problems of equity and distribution. My present point, however, is not the political implications of Nietzsche's view, but his innocence of politics. The knowledge and science he talks about are states of mind of individual persons, wholly private phenomena whose social implications are left largely unexplored; while his notion of 'life', too, alternates between the private and the cosmic spheres, leaving out the social and political which, Nietzsche believes, are either governed by the individual will or made ungovernable by the democratic mob.

Science, then, and the pursuit of knowledge are not 'absolutes'. They are approved when they further the cause of 'life' and denounced when they encroach upon it, *not* because they lead to truth, but because they lead to the great life-enhancing illusion called 'truth'. (Pontius Pilate, it appears, is the only real *gentleman* mentioned in the Gospels, *A* § 46.) And if there are truths which destroy life, then this too is part of that cosmic economy – the cosmos not of 'Being' but of 'becoming' – whereby the greater will lives and expands at the cost of the lesser.

Life cannot be defined: to define it would be to subordinate it to reason, its servant. This logical conundrum turned out to have most disreputable consequences. It was handed down to Nietzsche from Schopenhauer, and from Nietzsche to Alfred Rosenberg, to Ernst Jünger in the twenties, Gottfried Benn in the early thirties, and a host of other influential German authors. It takes the form of the following syllogism: (1) take x to be a man's 'intelligible character', his 'will', or 'will to power' or blood', or indeed anything postulated as *fundamental* to the being of man; (2) take y to be reason, or analytical reason, or criticism, or anything described as degenerate, pallid or hypercritical; then (3) any attempt to define x by y must fail because x is (said to be) the basis, or root, or ground ('Urgrund') of y, and it is clearly impossible to explain or define the fundamental by means of its derivative, the primary by means of the secondary. (The fallacy of the argument derives from the notion of misplaced concreteness, as though x and y had different physical depths.)

Life cannot be defined, yet the claim made on its behalf is supreme. Without life there are no values, no knowledge, and no 'will to power' either, and so it follows that all these – knowledge, values, the will and personal being of man – must be seen as relative to it. The argument is irresistibly circular: the ideals of nobility are those which enhance and sustain life, while life is that which is enhanced and sustained by the true and authentic – the highest ideals . . . Can we get no further?

Nietzsche is a Protestant philosopher. Beyond truth there is, for him, truthfulness. And we can get at least a little further in our argument by recognizing that the essential 'relativeness' or 'perspectivism'[5] of his moral scheme (and of his other schemes too) is the sign of a mind that is attempting to respond as appropriately – as truthfully – as possible to each new set of circumstances, and turns the strenuousness of its perspectivism into the supreme value.

There is a family likeness about the answers we get to the question, 'What is the value of values?' The value of truth is no more than equal to the value of illusion; the will is not a single thing but a series of inclinations determined by a flux of circumstances, the singularity of its name being no more than a linguistic and therefore practical convenience – a useful lie; the value of both esoteric and exoteric knowledge depends on the worth of the recipient and on what he makes of it; we perceive crudely and inaccurately, in distorting perspectives, and our language fails to reproduce even the prime colours, let alone the hues and shades, of our experience; the truth is supremely hard to get at and its value is relative to the difficulty of its pursuit, or again to the suffering which that pursuit entails; good is no good unless it is tested against overwhelming odds, value is valueless when it is asserted by another; moral precepts are not precepts unless they are generalized, and they cease to be worth obeying as soon as they are; compassion is weakness in one situation, strength in another; love is an aristocratic virtue, or again, a decadent romantic sickness; history is debilitating, or again a source of myth and strength; nihilism is the nether end of decadence, or winter's last throes before spring sets in . . . There seems to be no end to those apparent or partial contradictions, all of them illustrative of Nietzsche's insistence that the single man alone (and not fate, or a god, or society) is the bestower of values; that the personal being of man must determine what is valuable, and not the agreement of many; and that the insights he can achieve are not 'subjective' ('the subject', too, being a mere linguistic convenience), but relative and perspectivist [*WP* § 567]:

> It is the perspectivist mode that determines the [world's] character of 'appearance'. As if there were a world left over once you have taken away that perspective! Were you to do that, you would take away relativity!

'Life' is a repudiation of all that is sick and near to death, it is cruel toward all that is weak and old in us and around us, a perpetual struggle waged always at the expense of another life [*WP* § 369], it is impious toward the dying, and perpetually murderous. Its concern is not with distinctions but with antagonisms. It is not merely beyond good and evil, but also beyond all assent and denial [*WP* § 331], beyond all distinction of inner and outer, of form and matter, all logical finicking [*TS* II § 4] – yet reason *and* logic are among the fictitious procedures whereby life maintains itself. The assent to life entails the destruction of morality, which is nothing but the 'instinct to negate life' [*WP* § 343]. Life is the enduring form of all the processes in which force manifests itself and in which different contenders grow unequally; it is the attempt to encompass and subjugate as much as is in its power, and it derives pleasure and a sense of well-being from that process alone. It is at odds with consciousness [*WKG* V/2 pp. 401-2]: indeed, consciousness is only possible to the extent that it misunderstands and misinterprets the nature of life – 'the ultimate truth about the flux of all things [which is life] cannot be bodied forth, our organs (for life) are programmed for error . . . Life is the condition of knowledge. Error and delusion are the conditions of life – I mean the most profound errors. To know them is not to be rid of them.'

Because perpetual hostility between life and consciousness is the rule in the world we inhabit, and because in the struggle between life and knowledge the victory is never in doubt, 'truth is the kind of error without which a certain species of being would not be able to live – it is the *value for life* that ultimately decides.' [*WP* § 493] Yet because 'contradictions can be thought' [*WKG* V/2 pp. 401-2], Nietzsche experiments with the opposite idea, embracing very nearly the ethos of the modern scientist, and thus, incidentally, wiping out most of the arguments I have quoted:

Life has not disappointed me! Year by year I find it truer,
more desirable, more mysterious – from the day when the
great liberating thought dawned upon me that life may
well be an experiment of the knower – and not a duty nor
a predicament nor a swindle! And as for knowledge :
whatever it may mean for others – a bed of idleness, for
instance, or a road to a bed of idleness, an amusement
or idle pastime – for me it is a world of perils and victories,
where heroic feelings too have their arena and playground.
Life is a means to knowledge – with this maxim in one's
heart one can live bravely and even joyfully! [*JS* § 324]

But if life is all these things, what is *not* life? The only
thing it is not is *Being*, for if there were such a thing, it
would be the arrest of the eternal process of *becoming*;
though life exploits even this mendacious doctrine of Being
in order to make the idea of an eternal flux endurable,
for there is no end to the deceptions, chimeras and ruses
that life has learned to enjoy for its own mysterious
purposes.

There can be no doubt that even though Nietzsche's
conception of life as a warlike process owes something
to Heraclitus, it owes a good deal more to Darwin and
his followers. Why then is his attitude to Darwinism consistently hostile? Why does he call it 'true but lethal'
[*TS* II § 9]?

Both Nietzsche and Darwin ignore the distinction between the many and the one, though on opposite grounds :
Darwin to favour the many, Nietzsche to celebrate the
one.

Where Darwin sees 'adaptation and development of the
species' brought about by sheer numbers, Nietzsche emphasizes the odds against the survival of complex living
structures – structures which are valuable in proportion

to being complex, and therefore supremely vulnerable [*WP* § 684/ii]. He is keenly aware of the catastrophic quality – 'the utter disorder' – of the history of man. If there is a purpose in creation, it lies not in the perfection of a natural order but in the autonomy of the self-determining creative individual: whatever is perpetuated in the form of a racial or tribal characteristic, by that token degenerates. The Darwinian hypothesis of an ineluctable law of biological progress is immoral (in terms of Nietzsche's 'supra-morality'), the true value of life lies in the chanciness and indeterminability of all that is exceptional. And yet: if 'the average type' can be bred, why not its enemy, genius? In the eighties, the time of *Zarathustra*, Nietzsche (here following Darwin) is taken with the Lamarckian theory that acquired moral and cultural characteristics can be bred: what turns him against the idea is not the suspicion that such an inheritance cannot be enduring. It is his conviction, first formulated in *Thoughts out of Season* [III § 5], that the distance between the self-conscious, self-determining individual and the rest of mankind is greater than the distance which separates ordinary mankind from the animal kingdom; this is *his* axiom.

Quantity, in Nietzsche's view, almost by definition imperils quality. When Darwin writes (in *The Descent of Man*) that a single man's sacrifice of his own life has no evolutionary significance, whereas 'a tribe [which included] many members who were always ready to give aid to each other and to sacrifice themselves for the common good, would be victorious over most other tribes; and this would be natural selection', Nietzsche passionately believes that, whether or not such biological moralizings are 'true', they are certainly 'lethal' to any idea of what *he* regards as the genuine enhancement of man:

Anti-Darwin. What surprises me most when I survey the great destinies of man is that I always see before me the opposite of what Darwin and his School see or want to see today: that is, selection working in favour of the stronger, the better-constituted, and the progress of the species. The opposite is palpably the case: happy accidents are eliminated, the more highly evolved types lead nowhere, it is the average and below average types which ineluctably ascend to power . . . That will to power in which I recognize the ultimate basis and character of all change furnishes us with the explanation of why selection does not operate in favour of exceptional and fortunate cases: the strongest and most fortunate are weak when they are opposed by the organized instinct of the herd, the timidity of the weak, the greater number. My total picture of the world of values shows that in the highest values which rule mankind today it is not the happy accidents, the selected types, who have the upper hand; on the contrary, it is the types in whom decadence is rife – perhaps there is nothing so interesting in the world as this unwelcome spectacle . . . [*WP* § 685]

Survival, duration, numbers, biological usefulness – these are the enemies of Nietzsche's vision. The only value that matters is excellence issuing from catastrophe and deprivation, and proved in solitude and singularity, in the exception. Apart from that consistent emphasis on conflict, the 'life' that Nietzsche extols has nothing in common with the life which his Victorian contemporary had attempted to explain by giving Biology the intelligence of a purposeful God.

II The Will to Power

'Contradictions', Nietzsche says, 'can be thought', but they yield no coherent insight, for there is no limit to the implications that can be drawn from them. His reflections give us a series of vivid sketches of the moral problems that occupy him, but they provide no answer to that question to which he cannot help constantly returning – the question whether 'life' is to be regarded as an end and value in itself or as a means to some other end; and it is in this sense that 'life', amidst the countless scenes and descriptions he sets up for it, remains undefined and indefinable. As Nietzsche's religious views are centred round an absent deity, as his linguistic theory presents the elements of language in their relation to a silent centre, so his conception of moral values is related to a centre, named 'life', whose status and meaning remain a series of questions.

Yet there is no doubt that a fervent moral concern informs Nietzsche's criticisms of the customary morality of 'good and evil' as well as his attempts to go beyond it. If 'life' – the being of man in time – does not provide a valid scheme, it must be sought in life's chief constituent, the discontinuous and catastrophic will to power, whose moral concomitant is the personal authenticity of man. There is no doubt that here for once Nietzsche's aim is a systematic doctrine.

The principle of authenticity as a moral value is stated on a number of occasions, from the time of his essay on Schopenhauer in 1874 [*TS* III § 1] to *Ecce Homo* and the last notes of 1888:

> What does your conscience say? – 'You shall become that you are.'[6]

Nietzsche takes this formulation from the Second Ode of Pindar, but leaves his reader wondering whether it may not also contain a half-mocking, half-serious reference to the voice Moses heard in the burning bush, calling 'I am that I am'. However that may be, Nietzsche's meaning with its idiosyncratically religious overtone is clear, and entirely familiar. He is saying that the only absolute imperative a man should obey is that of his inward potential: whatever it is given to a man to become, *that* should indicate the direction, and be the goal, of his intense striving, his will. Authenticity is the deliberate coincidence of what a man is with what he can become. In the context Nietzsche gives it, and seen as he wants it to be seen, as a moral principle, Pindar's apophthegm becomes a validation of the self by the simple process of self-realization through seriousness and single-mindedness. To put it in the jargon of yesterday: it becomes the maxim of the doctrine of 'commitment'.

'Commitment' to what? This is a question Nietzsche does not ask. And when his existentialist disciples say, in effect, 'It does not matter: the choice of a gratuitous object or of an absurd task is better than no choice at all', Nietzsche may not agree, but he provides no ground on which to oppose them. 'Become that you are': this reduplication of the 'I' is emptiness itself. Not only does it not offer any guarantee of the moral quality of the 'I' that is thus being confirmed, but it sets up the quality of 'commitment', its intensity and earnestness, as the dominant *moral* quality and the criterion of good and evil. Of course, it is true to the point of banality that what Nietzsche has in mind is 'commitment' to a valuable goal: 'Your true self . . . lies immeasurably above that which you usually take to be your self,' [*TS* III § 1] it being understood (for reasons that will become clear in the next chapter) that 'your usual self' is your social self and

77

therefore 'inauthentic'. But is it not equally possible that 'your true self' may lie immeasurably *below* 'your usual self', and that society, its conventions and laws, may mercifully prevent its realization? Moreover, if authenticity is *the* dominant moral category, what criteria are left for 'high' and 'low'? Nietzsche rightly ridicules the Victorian hope that a new morality, which has freed itself from a transcendental Christian sanction, should turn out to be very much the same as the morality previously attached to Christianity,[7] yet he does not stop to consider the necessary limits of any conceivable moral reform, and thus the inevitable overlap between old and new.

Like Marxism, his idea of authenticity lives on the Jewish and Christian moral capital he disowns. His remarkable description of 'the great deceivers' shows up the full ambiguity of the doctrine. Read by itself, it must be one of the finest portraits of the religious or political demagogue we have, even more relevant to our century than to Nietzsche's own:

> In all great deceivers a remarkable process is at work, to which they owe their power. In the very act of deception with all its preparations, the dreadful voice and face and gestures, amid the whole effective scenario they are overcome by *their belief in* themselves; and it is this belief which then speaks so miraculously, so persuasively, to their audience . . . For men believe in the truth of all that is seen to be firmly believed. [*HAH* I § 52]

But in what way does *this* 'belief in oneself' differ from the belief Nietzsche commends in the context of 'You shall become that you are'? His moral intention – the intention to expose fanaticism and the histrionics of false belief – in this and similar sketches is not in doubt. In one of the

central arguments of *Antichrist* [§ 53f] he warns us that
readiness for martyrdom has nothing to do with the truth
of a cause; that men like Savonarola, Luther, Rousseau,
Robespierre and Saint-Simon are no better than 'sick spirits,
epileptics of the concept'; that strong beliefs are prison-
houses of the mind; and that '*to have* a conviction or a
belief . . . is . . . a Carlylism', is not to belong to oneself
but to be a means to another man's purpose. And in the
same reflection [§ 54] in which he tells us that he does
not like the sinister mien of the fanatic he also complains
that 'men prefer seeing gestures (the fanatic's gestures) to
hearing reasons' . . . Yet what *reason* is there for holding
that the alternative to belief, 'the great passion' [A § 54]
which Nietzsche identifies with the total person, is necessarily good? Why should *being* a scoundrel be better than
acting one? He seems unaware that he is giving us nothing
to distinguish the fanaticism that goes with bad faith from
his own belief in the unconditioned value of self-realization and self-becoming – that is, from his own belief in
the Superman. We for our part are bound to look askance
at this questionable doctrine. We can hardly forget that
the solemn avowal of this reduplicated self – the pathos of
personal authenticity – was the chief tenet of fascism and
national socialism. No man came closer to the full realization of self-created 'values' than A. Hitler.

But to say this is not enough. The fascist ideologists
were not some obscure flat-earth cranks. With the demise
of a religiously sanctioned morality and of its successor,
the morality of duty, Nietzsche's conception of authenticity – of 'to thine own self be true' – represents a con-
summation of the secular searching for values which is
central to the recent intellectual and political history of
the West.[8] Only because it was so central could the totalitarian régimes justly claim that they were fulfilling the

79

'authentic' aspirations of intellectuals and 'the people' alike.

'The will to power', the cardinal concept of Nietzsche's only systematic venture, is intended as the centre-piece of a vast philosophical panorama; to its working-out he devoted the greater part of the last four years of his active life. He presents it as a principle discernible in all nature, in accordance with which a self or 'centre of power' expands beyond its own boundaries, asserts itself over another and strives to appropriate it. It is precisely what Dr Johnson has in mind when, 'on his favourite subject of subordination', and in defiance of all Whiggish nonsense, he proclaims, 'So far is it from being true that men are naturally equal, that no two people can be half an hour together, but one *shall acquire* an evident superiority over the other.'[9]

The will to power is the agency whereby man, 'the weakest, cleverest being' [*WP* § 856], becomes master of the earth, yet it is not identical with life. If for Schopenhauer the 'will to life' was the fundamental principle of all being, Nietzsche challenges this view by arguing that where there is no 'life' there can be no 'will' either [Z II § 12]. 'Life', accordingly, appears as an amorphous, in-choate thing which must have a direction and purpose imposed upon it: the will to power becomes the impulse behind *distinct* activities. Its realization in nature[10] as well as in history, in the rise and fall of worldly and spiritual institutions, provides man with the horizon necessary to sustain life itself, but it is equally to be seen as the motive behind all individual cultural, artistic and religious activity. It is the force at work behind all our valuations, behind the 'perspectivism' of our interpretations of the world, and behind the great philosophical fictions: 'To stamp the character of *Being* on the process of *becoming* – that is the highest will to power.' [*WP* § 617] It is the impulse behind the acquisition, ordering and creation of knowledge, and behind creativity itself. Logic, too, including the law of contradiction, and our 'forms of cognition',[11] are manifestations of whatever happens to be the victorious form of willing at any one time, for we are motivated, not by a 'will to truth', but by the 'will to render the world thinkable' [Z II § 12]. And in a reflection that is usually printed at the very end of *The Will to Power* [§ 1067], Nietzsche writes:

> This world . . . my *Dionysian* world of eternal self-creation and eternal self-destruction, this mystery world of twofold voluptuous delight, my 'beyond good and evil', without goal unless the joy of the circle is a goal, without will unless it is the circle's good will toward itself – do you want a *name* for this world? A *solution* of all its riddles? A *light* for you too, you who are the best concealed, the strongest, the most intrepid, the most midnightly of men? *This world is the will to power and nothing else besides*. And you too are that will to power, and nothing else besides.

'And nothing else besides'? It is certainly true that as soon as we try to see human conduct in the light of this single principle, a multitude of insights opens up. We find that the 'will to power' is involved in every political activity and (if the confessions of our scientists are anything to go by) in the sciences as well; it colours the whole gamut of our feelings and emotions, and is present in every social and familial context. It is hard to think of a mundane situation in which it is not present: a quarrel between two friends about an ascertainable fact, the contest inherent in every erotic encounter and in the sex-act itself; the functions of the teacher, the preacher, the boss, the adviser are unthinkable without involving the exercise of power – but also that of the benefactor and alms-giver of every kind, the man who 'loves to surprise', who 'gladly forgives', the superior conversationalist à la Dr Johnson, the man who shames you by his misfortune, let alone the one who shames you by being on top of the world. Nor is there any doubt about the 'supra-*moral*' nature of all these insights. The principle, if applied (as Nietzsche proposes to apply it) as a critique of our customary notions of good and evil, enables us to discriminate between different actions according to the strength or weakness of the will involved in these actions. For if we now ask what is *not* to be identified as this 'will to power' – what, in this scheme, is a 'non-value' – the answer (like the answer to the question, What is *not* 'life'?) will be: all forms of passive response to the expansive nature of the will, that is, all forms of decadence, tiredness and despair. In the human sphere Nietzsche calls this resistance 'Ressentiment', by which he means a reactive grudgingness whose endless, 'eternal' chronicle is all of human history. But to acknowledge the illuminating insights which the principle of 'the will to power' vouchsafes is still very far from accepting it as the total explanatory principle of existence in the world.

For if it really is the monistic explanation Nietzsche proclaims it to be, how are we to account for the sheer variety of the phenomena in which this will 'objectifies' itself – that variety in the detailed descriptions of which Nietzsche excels? Is it really convincing to claim that a man's loving, caring, instructing, finding out and reflecting do not merely involve 'the will to power' but are 'nothing else besides'? It is not difficult to accept 'the will to power' as a disposition of mind aiming at the subjugation of any object outside myself; but if this *ob*ject, this *Gegen*stand, too, is to be seen as a product of that will, we are stuck in the Idealist's trap of a solipsistic universe.

But this is not the only argument Nietzsche fails to pursue to whatever consequences it might lead.

Instead of pressing this logical point, let us turn once again to Nietzsche's favourite mode of thought, the historical: we shall find that here, too, the monism does not work. If there is anything in the recent 'Nietzschean' era that comes close to an embodiment of 'the will to power', it is Hitler's life and political career; and this is so even if we assume (as we have good reason for assuming) that Nietzsche's imagination falls far short of this reality. The abstruse and unhistorical subterfuges Marxist and Freudian interpreters are put to when attempting to isolate the major motive force of politics generally, and Hitler in particular, leave little doubt that Nietzsche's identification of the 'will to power' is a good deal more direct and convincing. The neglect of the Nietzschean analysis – the unwillingness to believe that *the desire for destructive power* is a major human motive – has led and perhaps still leads Western liberal politicians to underestimate the sheer intensity of the struggle in societies whose legal and constitutional arrangements they like to regard as old-fashioned.

Yet there is in Hitler (and men like him) a destructiveness at work which goes beyond any conceivable assertion or expansion of the self, beyond any will to *power*, to the point of a 'will-to-nothingness' which is wholly negative. Is this 'Wille in's Nichts' [*WP* § 55], which Nietzsche sees rising up at the moment 'when all existence has lost its "meaning"', an extension of the 'will to power' and therefore redeemable by it; or is it an independent principle, rather like Freud's 'Thanatos principle'? The question, left open by Nietzsche, is of considerable importance in his prognosis for European history. He conceives the 'will to power' as the heir to Western decadence, but only if it is the all-encompassing monistic principle of Being can it also be seen as a redemption from nihilism. It is because they saw it in these terms, as disease and cure alike, that countless German intellectuals espoused national socialism, that ideology which promised the will's greatest unfolding. We know that this promise was false, and that the destructive will can operate as an independent principle, not redeemable by itself. Nietzsche did not know this clearly enough. The charge is that, not recognizing the will's destructiveness for the unredeemable thing it is, he did not envisage its full consequences. He anticipates the future: not, however, as a true prophet, but as one of its accomplices.

The attempt has been made to salvage this 'will to power' for traditional moral philosophy by claiming that Nietzsche conceived of it as 'the will to overcome oneself'.[12] This would place him squarely in the same tradition as St Paul, Spinoza and Schopenhauer, though it would then be hard to see what was so original, or notorious, about his moral ideas. Now it is true that 'the will to power' does not necessarily take the form of the master-slave relationship, but includes 'sacrifice and service and amorous glances' among its subterfuges [Z II § 12]. Indeed, this 'power' need not be conceived in any such barbaric ways as the Italian and French fascists and the German national socialists conceived of it (though it is absurd to deny that the intellectual superstructure of these political movements is as inconceivable without Nietzsche's ideas as these movements are without their superstructure). It is also true that this 'will' does not necessarily entail the actual physical or psychic destruction of, or encroachment on, another will, since Nietzsche is sometimes content to identify it with 'a feeling of increase and power' which needs no confirmation from overt violence. It does entail a self-overcoming, but only where wantonness, cupidity and the like act as impediments to its full exercise: 'Only the degenerate [regard] . . . annihilation, castration [and other such violent means] as indispensable', for they are too weak-willed to practise moderation [*TI* V § 2]. But when he writes [*WKG* V/1 p. 687] that, contrary to 'what the Germans think', strength need not 'reveal itself in hardness and cruelty' and that it may reside 'in mildness and stillness', Nietzsche is not offering an alternative to the 'will to power', but is on the contrary suggesting that the principle of conquest is no more confined to a crude show of force than it was to 'the dreadful voice and face and gestures' of the false prophet and demagogue. Conquest remains at the heart of the doctrine. Only where it finds no opposition is the 'will to power' not destructive.

There is a 'will to truth', a 'will to knowledge', and a will which is instrumental in the creating of values, yet they are all deemed decadent unless they are subordinated to the enhancement of the self. The purpose of all self-overcoming that is not decadent is the validation of command: every Judaic or Christian 'thou shalt' is to be translated into 'I will'. Self-overcoming in the service of a moral or spiritual law (as in Christian or Kantian morality) or in the service of a common good is rejected, and so is the idea of self-overcoming for its own sake: wherever a lower self is overcome for the sake of a higher self, 'wherever there is decline and the falling of leaves, there life is sacrificing itself for the sake of power!' [*Z* II § 12].

By designating the 'will to power' as the ultimate good, Nietzsche is not, of course, going 'beyond good and evil'; is not (as he claimed) constructing an 'amoralism'. He is making of that 'will' the principle of a moral doctrine for the enhancement of an elect self as a means to the enhancement of a similarly elect portion of mankind – but

Nietzsche is not interested in how the transition from the self to mankind is to be effected.

Here if anywhere is Nietzsche's positive system of metaphysics. It arises at the point where the 'will to power' (which is his greatest single reflective experiment) is identified with value judgements (which are the inveterate consistency of his thinking).

Among a number of possible modes of being, man's being in this, his only world is inextricably involved in valuations: being *is* the setting up of tables of values and judging in accordance with them.[18] They in turn are products of man's willing: manifestations of the 'will to power', they are created by the master, accepted and obeyed by the slaves. Whatever is valuable (because constituted in relationships dominated by the strongest will) is true. There is no other truth. But if there is no other truth than that which relates to the things and people in the world (and they are 'always in relationship'), how can we know that the idea and system of an all-encompassing 'will' are true? How can man, the agent of any one specific 'will to power', know it in its metaphysical totality?

A quandary very much like this was bequeathed to Nietzsche by Schopenhauer,[14] who 'solved' it by postulating in man a unity of perceiving subject with perceived object, and declared this unity to be mystical and all-encompassing. Nietzsche is too honest for such subterfuges. What wrecks his hopes for a grand system and saves him from getting stuck with a monstrous unworkable principle is his intellectual honesty, which is full of the seeds of self-destruction; when it forces him to break his own 'system' asunder, he will not hesitate to do so:

What if *either* the hypothesis of the 'will to power' ceases to be adequate [*WKG* V/1 pp. 415-6] because it

turns out to be 'a metaphor that can mislead' [*WKG* VIII/
3 p. 186], a mere reification [*Mus* XVI p. 61] of very
diverse phenomena which are better considered separately;
or the conclusion becomes inevitable that the pursuit of
knowledge is an end and principle in its own right, so
much so that life itself turns out to be 'a means of
knowledge and an experiment of the knower' [*JS* IV §
324]? Is knowledge one of the agents of the 'will to
power', or the 'will to power' one of the objects of knowledge? No answer that Nietzsche gives to these questions
remains uncontradicted.

The doctrine of the 'will to power' as it emerges from the
convolute of Nietzsche's notes cannot be accommodated
within any non-catastrophic, eudaemonic scheme. Whether
its notion of power is subtle or crude, concrete or
abstract, it remains a doctrine of conquest and embattled
domination. It is certainly not an invitation to self-
indulgence in any ordinary sense. At their most consistent,
Nietzsche's reflections point in the opposite direction,
away from all comfort. And the bleak values which will
receive his assent cannot be described as 'a striving to
transcend and perfect oneself',[15] unless it be a perfecting
for death.

Nietzsche is not patient enough to draw out the full
implications of his thinking – nor is he inert enough to let
it come to rest. He feels compelled to move from one
experiment to the next, from one provisional solution to
the next, because he 'writes so well' [*EH* III] – because
the very mode of his writing, the energy and versàtility
of his pen, will not let him stay and be dull. But what
alternative to 'the will to power' is there?

III   The God-less Theology

We return to the central question of Nietzsche's moral enquiry: What principle or scheme will yield an adequate description *and* norm of man's being in the world, will 'bring out the best in him'? What is man's best?

Certainly the answer will be related to Nietzsche's Protestant Christianity, for it is bound to take issue with the religious situation of his age, which is for him 'the age of the death of God', and with the morality of that age, which is for him the morality of decadence. It will look very much *like* a religious scheme (and many of Nietzsche's disciples will regard it as such), yet its religiousness will be full of paradox and riven by conflict. It will make no claims to being perennially valid, but instead emphasize its own historicity. An exclusively private device, it will allow no value to politics or to any of the institutional safeguards men put between themselves and the crack of doom. It will contain no moral absolutes or material imperatives ('do this, do not do that!'), yet it must enjoin one way of doing things in preference to others. And finally, while it cannot help being a scheme, *a generalization*, it will strive to keep to the language of 'little facts and inconspicuous truths' [*HAH* I § 3], and to preserve the intuition that 'every action is unique and incommensurable with every other action' [*JS* IV § 335].

Does all this not look uncommonly like that 'phantasmagoria' which Nietzsche saw at the heart of every comprehensive philosophical system?[16] Besides, considering how much variety and how many living colours Nietzsche imparts to his discrete reflections, why bother about a 'scheme', the mere corpse of a summary?

Because, whether we choose to call it a moral system, a *Weltanschauung*, or merely a certain style of moral thought and action, what we are now considering is Nietzsche's bequest to the new century, is a single distinct heritage of moral-existential attitudes.

The premise on which this scheme rests anticipates our deep discontent with the industrial world and its values. In the spring of 1888 he writes:

> What I attack is that economic optimism which behaves as though, with the increasing *expenditure* of all, the *welfare* of all would also necessarily increase. To me the opposite seems to be the case: the sum total of the expenditure of all amounts to a total loss: *man is diminished* – indeed, one no longer knows what purpose this immense process has served in the first place. A purpose? A new purpose – that is what mankind needs! [*WP* § 866]

If man is to be saved from the inauthenticity and decadence he calls civilized life, his 'new purpose' must be relative to its being supremely difficult of attainment, it must be on the border-line of the unattainable; while conversely, anything that is not attained at such an exorbitant cost cannot be the real thing at all. We may call this Nietzsche's 'morality of strenuousness', his 'dear purchase' or, in a phrase from *Zarathustra*, the morality of 'the spirit of gravity', where the German word, 'Geist der *Schwere*', conjures up a gamut of physical and mental phenomena, from 'ponderousness' through 'recalcitracy' to 'hardness' and 'difficulty'. A man's value, accordingly, lies in his readiness to undertake whatever are to him the most strenuous and least comforting moral and existential tasks, regardless of their accepted moral value. The 'purpose' or salvation of modern man (like 'Grace' in an earlier argument, the Christian term is both inappropriate and impossible to avoid) is to be purchased at the highest, most exacting price he can conceive of; and perhaps it lies beyond – tantalizingly, it may be, just beyond – what a man can pay with his entire being and existence. The structure of any genuine theology is reversed: instead of a relative personal effort being 'justified' by an absolute end, an existential effort is made absolute so as to 'justify' a relative end. Christian theology is replaced by the penitential theology of a God-less universe.

This, then, is Nietzsche's *experimentum in corpore vili*, the one morality that cuts to the quick. Formulations of it occur throughout his career, yet he never seems aware how consistent – and destructive – an attitude these formulations represent. After the declaration (see above p. 60) that 'the goal of mankind cannot lie in its end but in its highest specimens' (1874), he goes on to exhort his contemporaries:

> . . . find an exalted and noble *raison d'être* in life: seek out destruction for its own sake! I know of no better purpose in life than to be destroyed by that which is great and impossible! [*TS* II § 9]

– as though its impossibility were what makes his 'ideal' great. Again, in the Wagner essay two years later, he commends the cultural and pedagogic function of Bayreuth and offers its tragic masterpieces as lessons to those who are 'preparing for death in the fight for justice and love' [*TS* IV § 4], as though only death could validate their cause.[17] Youthful romantic rhetoric? The self-destructive strenuousness of this strange morality never changes. When Nietzsche writes (to Seydlitz, 11 June 1878) that he wishes his life to reflect 'my views about morality and art (the hardest things that my sense of truth has so far wrung from me)'; when he proclaims, in the 1886 preface to *Human, All-Too-Human,*

> I now took sides *against* myself and *for* everything that would hurt me and would come hard to me . . . ;

when, in *Beyond* (1886) he writes:

> A thing might be true, even though it were noxious and dangerous in the highest degree – indeed, it might be fundamental to the nature of existence that we perish by the full knowledge of it; so that the strength of a human spirit might be measured by how much truth it could be made to bear . . . ;

when, in the notes to *The Will to Power* (1887-8) he defines 'virtue' as 'the delight we take in opposition', adding that

> I assess the power of [a man's] will by how much resistance, pain and torment it can endure and turn to its advantage . . . ; [§ 382]

we are left in no doubt that this 'experimental philosophy which I live', represents Nietzche's most intimate personal undertaking and purpose, and informs every phase of his creative life. Its fullest expression is to be found in *Thus Spoke Zarathustra,* the book on which he pinned his highest hopes.

Why does Nietzsche choose the Old Persian prophet, Zoroaster, to act the part of Christ in this strange parody of the Gospels? Because Zarathustra is the founder of the earliest dualistic Aryan religion we know – 'he who first saw that the moving wheel at the centre of all things is the battle between good and evil' – and therefore shall be the prophet who proclaims the end of the rule of good and evil [*EH* last section]. After ten years in a mountainous solitude Zarathustra decides to go down among men:

> But when he came into the forest, suddenly there stood before him an old man who had left his holy abode to look for roots in the woods . . .
> 'And what is the holy man doing in the forest?' asked Zarathustra.
> The holy man answered: 'I make songs and sing them, and when I make songs I laugh, I cry and I hum: in this way I praise God. With singing, crying, laughing and humming I praise the god who is my God. But what gift do you bring us?'
> When Zarathustra had heard these words, he bade the holy man farewell and said: 'What have I to give you? Nay, let me go, lest I take something away from you!'
> And so they separated, the old one and the man, laughing as two boys laugh.
> But when Zarathustra was alone, he spoke thus to his heart: Is it possible that the holy old man in his forest has not yet heard the news that God is dead? [Z introduction]

This 'death' of the Christian God Nietzsche identifies with the virtual end of the morality of good and evil, and of all forms of idealism. It is for him the cardinal event of modern history and of the contemporary world, the ghost that looms behind his every important thought. It is impossible to imagine what his writings would be like 'were it not that I have bad dreams'.

That his religious reflections are not neutral, no mere *constatations*, hardly needs emphasizing at this stage. Here

more than anywhere else he consciously [*GM* I §§ 2-3]
exploits the performative function of 'prophetic' utterance. His intention is not merely to announce the end of
religion but by his rhetoric to help bring it about: 'whatever is falling – let's give it a push, too!' [Z III § 12] What
then are Nietzsche's criticisms of the faith in which he
was reared? Before returning to *Zarathustra* and its
peculiar theology, we must consider the rejection from
which it arises.

For Schopenhauer, the mid-nineteenth century is 'an age
in which religion is almost entirely dead' and when 'the
shares of the old Jew are falling'; Heinrich Heine's rhetoric
is more dramatic but equally irreverent: 'Our heart is full
of terrible pity,' he writes in 1852. 'It is the old Jehovah
himself preparing for death . . . Can you hear the ringing
of the bell? Kneel down, they are bringing the sacraments
to a dying God.' These are the antecedents of that lurid
and notorious phrase used by Nietzsche for the first time
in § 108 of the third book of *The Joyous Science* (spring
1882) and then again, four years later, at the opening of
the fifth and last section of that book: 'The greatest event
of recent times – that "God is dead", that the belief in the
Christian God is no longer tenable – is beginning to cast
its first shadows over Europe.' Now [*D* § 95] he presents
it as a simple fact of modern life, and rejoices in its consequences. His anti-religious and atheist argument is based
on the view, set up and illustrated in countless reflections
in the books of the middle period, that the belief in God
results in an impoverishment of men's lives; that the
compensatory belief in heaven ('the Land of Back and
Beyond') reduces the value and dignity of physical existence; that the belief in personal immorality, apart from
being intolerably egalitarian [*A* § 43], diminishes the

seriousness of men's experience of irretrievable time by mythologizing time into a spurious perpetuity called 'eternity'; that Christianity preaches a denigration of the life of the senses and thus leads to a fanatical contempt for 'what is real in the world'. All that Nietzsche attacks is formulated in one of Kafka's 'Meditations': 'Nothing exists but the spiritual world. That which we call the sensuous world is the evil in the spiritual.'

There is a Manichean trend to Nietzsche's arguments: polemically exaggerating the world-contemning nature of Christianity, he has nothing to say in recognition of the joyful, positive nature of that faith of which Christ said, 'My yoke is easy, and my burden is light' (*Matt.* 11/30). He says next to nothing about the *pietas loci* which (as Hölderlin's poems show) is an essential part of the Gospels and of the Christian world picture. He seems to be unaware of the overwhelming debt which every form of Western art owes, not only to the Christian faith, but to the Church in which that faith has its historical being. And he has nothing to say about the positive meaning of Christ's incarnation (1. *Joh.* 4/9) as a validation of our mortality.

To these objections Nietzsche would no doubt reply that they are irrelevant, for *his* remarks are not concerned with the perennial possibilities of the Christian faith but with its actual contemporary desuetude. Put in these terms, his charge is more considerable. It is that, in his day and age, the belief in God is dispensable because the presence or absence of faith in men's minds no longer makes any real difference to the lives they lead, to the world in which they live.

What is it that Christianity calls 'the world'? To be a soldier, a judge, a patriot; to defend oneself; to look to one's honour; to seek one's advantage; *to be proud*:

every practice of every moment, every instinct and every valuation translated into action is today anti-Christian. [*A* § 38]

Can we deny that this is a convincing reading of the signs of the times, Nietzsche's times and ours? And equally convincing, it seems to me, is his explanation of the religious decline. Leaving to one side the Victorian clichés about the conflict between faith and science, he draws from the very denunciation of Christianity a paradoxical acknowledgement of its historical significance. This is the dialectical tension that informs *The Genealogy of Morals* (July 1887). For here he recognizes that 'science' – the body of stable and accurate knowledge to the accumulation of which men devote their lives – far from being the antagonist of faith and of the religious outlook, owes its origins and development to Christian thinking and ideals. He singles out truthfulness as the basic disposition of mind which informs every uncompromising pursuit of knowledge; and, recognizing this truthfulness as an essentially Christian virtue, he sees the decline of religion as the radical consequence of its own religiously inspired morality: 'All great things' – but we must not pretend that Nietzsche always sees Christianity as 'great' – 'All great things perish by their own agency, by an act of self-cancellation.' ['Selbstaufhebung', *GM* III § 27]

Christian truthfulness (he concludes) is not fundamentally different from the spirit that has informed Western philosophy since the days of Socrates, that decadent proto-Christian and first martyr in the cause of his own questionable convictions [*TI* II]. But the 'will to truth' which informs Christianity (and Western philosophy) is in the service of ascetic ideals – ideals which seek to uphold a sickly and degenerate will to power over a healthy assertion of life, at the same time as they oppose art and 'the will to deception', and 'all other forms of illusion'. Throughout Western history, religion and philosophy have been weapons in the hands of the envious and the resentful, the unhappy and the self-haters – of all those who are afraid of life and 'wish to be different, wish they were elsewhere' [§ 13]: they make of truthfulness itself an anti-value.

Nietzsche's arguments are always at their weakest where he offers 'ways of becoming' as the grounds of value judgements. For even if it were true that the Christian priesthood is recruited from 'the underprivileged' and the Uriah Heeps (which Nietzsche elsewhere [D § 60] denies), and even if people could live more happily without religious beliefs, the double inference, that this renders religion worthless and the belief in God illusory, would still be unwarranted. Nietzsche's atheism at this point is 'fixed' and dogmatic: apart from the false inference there is only assertion. He merely denies – he does not attempt to disprove – a loving and merciful God, and Christ as the son of that God; and he axiomatically assumes that the meaning of life must be sought elsewhere. But in saying that because men do not believe in God, therefore he does not exist, 'is dead', Nietzsche is caught in the same solipsist-idealist trap in which his doctrine of the 'will to power' had landed him.

Taking no warning from Greek tragedy, Nietzsche has no fear of hubris [GM III § 9]. His ultimate indictment of Christian belief (the basis of his charge that it is against life and against the earth) is that Christianity does not recognize man as master of the universe since it insists that the freedom, authority and knowledge vouchsafed to men are all relative to an alien, outside decree, and rendered intolerable (to Nietzsche at all events) because they are derivative. Therefore, Nietzsche argues, man cannot reach the highest enhancement of his powers until he has destroyed in himself his belief in the divine. Only then will life have a meaning for him and the earth yield up her treasures to him. There is a tone of almost cheerful aggressiveness about many remarks in book III of *The Genealogy of Morals*, but it does not last. In the more or less contemporary notebooks, Nietzsche calls the end of religion 'the most terrible news': rather than cope with the 'unbearable loneliness' of their new condition (he writes there), men will seek out their shattered God, and for his sake they will love the very serpents that dwell among his ruins . . .[18] Yet the melodramatic metaphors obscure his vision. There are moments when he, like Freud in *The Future of an Illusion*, appears less clear about the human consequences of the end of faith than he is about the need to hasten the coming of that end. He wants the brave new world to be populated, not simply by the unconcerned, but by men who, while unconcerned about 'the death of God', will yet be metaphysically, religiously concerned. But what is this bladeless knife without a handle, this religious disposition without a God?

Our experience almost a century later suggests that the liberation Nietzsche hoped for has brought no freedom. Where men have abandoned their belief in an immortal soul, the destruction they visit on others has become more heedless and complete than it was before; and where they act in the conviction that 'nothing is true, everything is permitted' [*GM* III § 24] – that there is no authority to appeal to – their style of life is more troubled and more sordid than before.

The denigration of man's life on this earth and the subordination of man to God are Nietzsche's two principal objections to Christianity. The third is his attack on Christianity as scripture and dogma, and on the Church as an institutionalization of that dogma; and this attack is set in sharp contrast to a strange eulogy of Jesus of Nazareth.[19] The argument is conducted in the posthumously published *Antichrist*, written and completed between 9 September and 14 October 1888.

The title is misleading, perhaps deliberately so, and has little to do with the name traditionally given to Christ's enemy at his second coming. More relevant is Schopenhauer's use of the word to represent the view that the world has merely a physical significance: to deny the world its moral significance (Schopenhauer had argued) amounts to the greatest and most pernicious error of which the human mind is capable – such a denial is 'personified as Antichrist'.[20] This is the meaning Nietzsche invokes in his title, and occasionally for himself. Thus the book, intended as the first volume of a grand 're-valuation of all values', proposes an affirmation of anti-moral, anti-religious and anti-spiritual values. Incidentally, it is also Nietzsche's final rebuttal of Schopenhauer, the end of his life-long *agon*.

The Antichrist consists of a series of profound insights embedded in a mixture of vituperation and incongruities: but insights and incongruities alike derive from a single perspective (which I shall describe in the next chapter) – a rejection of that sphere of experience where 'two or three are gathered together'. Its opposite, Nietzsche's almost absolute individualism, is given freer rein than ever before.

Christianity now appears as the denial of all truth, instinctive and scientific alike. It is seen as a direct descendant of the Jewish theocratic state – at first a threat to the life of a small, deeply unheroic nation, and then a powerful weapon in that nation's lethal struggle against Rome. It is 'a diseased barbarism that sets itself up as

power' [§ 37], a falsification of everything Christ was and
stood for, and the very opposite of 'the Evangel', 'the good
tidings'. Its history Nietzsche sees as a series of ever
cruder misunderstandings of an original lofty symbolism:
'the very word "Christianity" is a misunderstanding –
the truth is, there was only one Christian and he died on
the cross'; and *'from that moment on'* all is lies [§ 39].
The pure, authentic vision of a naïve Jesus of Nazareth
has been corrupted – dogmatized and institutionalized –
by a fanatical rabbi who set out to restore the threatened
priestly power and conspiracy of the weak: Paul is the
prophet of the new 'Dysangelium'.

The distaste conveyed in this portrait of the first
Christian theologian has no parallel elsewhere in Nietzsche's writings. Paul is in every way Christ's opposite:
teacher of a nihilistic morality, a Jewish sea-lawyer and
upholder of a moribund legalism; his renunciation of the
Law (*Gal.* 3/24) is not mentioned. He is the inventor of
the doctrine of the Cross ('We – the rabble – are all on the
cross, therefore we are all divine'), the myth-maker of the
resurrection (a piece of 'rabbinical impudence'), and he is
the first to appeal to the twin authorities – both equally
unreasonable – of tradition and revolution. These (Nietzsche concludes) are Paul's means of securing Christianity's
victory over Rome. Now the invective broadens out to
include an account of the disastrous consequences of
Luther's protest, and the Renaissance joins Rome as a
missed opportunity for making 'the Great Life' victorious.
The pungent anti-Semitism of historical sketches earlier in
Antichrist is more or less cancelled out by an equally
telling anti-anti-Semitism: for two thousand years now
victory has been with 'the little Jews' of all nations and
races, who have the religious superlatives constantly on
their lips, and the sickly smile of the forgiving dévots . . .

To all this, the portrait of Jesus of Nazareth [A §§ 32-4] provides the starkest possible contrast. Nietzsche presents him largely in negative terms: Christ is no teacher, no priest, no prophet even; he belongs to no state, no culture and no religion or Church; nothing about him conveys the feeling that he is securely at home in our common world; even his words that have come down to us do not really matter – they are not a literal truth but 'merely a sign-language, mere semiotics'. Christ passes no judgement, has no will to resist or negate, to be angry or to hold anyone responsible. Incapable of denial and negation, he lives *outside* the world seen as *a world of contrasts*. He simply *is*. His 'kingdom of heaven' is not the Church's metaphysical cloud-cuckooland but 'a state of the heart'. Nietzsche is trying to portray one who is living 'the genuine evangelical practice' which, being outside history, 'is still possible even today':

> Using the phrase loosely, one could call Jesus 'a free spirit'
> – he cares nothing for all that is fixed. The word *kills*, all
> that is fixed *kills*. [A § 32]

It is hardly too much to say that this Jesus, too, is the 'Antichrist' of Nietzsche's title.

There are moments in this book (which is Nietzsche's strangest) when his understanding of Christian spirituality is as intimate as any Christian apologist's. Yet his portrait of Jesus amounts to a radical misinterpretation of the Gospels. When Nietzsche argues that Christ belongs to no religion, he is really saying that religion itself, as 'a particular *social* realization of a relationship to an absolute ground of meaning'[21] is a thing of no value. And when he portrays Jesus as one who knows no contrasts and passes no judgements, Nietzsche ignores the core of the New Testament, Christ's teaching of the great separation,[22] with all its parables of the sheep and the goats, the broad way and the narrow, the good fish and the refuse, the wise and the foolish virgins ...

And the source of this extravagant interpretation? Although Nietzsche ridicules [*A* § 53] the anti-theological tradition of 'the Pietists and other Swabian cows', his portrait of a 'gentle Jesus, meek and mild' is in fact part of that age-old German Pietist tradition[23] in which he was brought up (and which also informs the Nazarene, pre-Raphaelite school of painters in his time). But if Nietzsche's portrait of Jesus is a sentimental misunderstanding, his portrait of Paul, intended as a contrasting masterpiece of psychological finesse, is an absurdity. 'Whoever finds Paul repugnant and uncanny', writes Rudolf Bultmann, 'must find Jesus just as repugnant and uncanny.'[24]

What meaning have these portraits of the Nazarene Jesus and the Levantine Paul for Nietzsche in his search for a system of new values, announced in the preface of *The Antichrist*? Nietzsche calls Christ 'an interesting decadent' and himself 'a conscious decadent' [*CW* preface]; he calls Jesus, in Dostoyevsky's sense, an 'idiot',[25] and himself 'a fool' and 'a mountebank'. These self-identifications are as transparent as the self-repudiation contained in his caricature of Paul. It is as if Nietzsche's portrait of Paul were weighed down by all the gravity of judgement and mental turmoil to which he, Nietzsche, feels himself eternally condemned, while the portrait of Jesus has all the irenic and unstrenuous qualities of being from which he knows himself to be forever excluded. It is as a wish-fulfilment and absolution from a lifetime's exertion and consciousness of sin that this Nazarene Jesus, like a figure from a poem by Georg Trakl, stalks through the pages of *The Antichrist*, bypassing its vituperation, its contrasts and contradictions. It is a glimpse, no more, of the world seen 'as an aesthetic phenomenon'.

Returning now to *Thus Spoke Zarathustra*, we recognize it as the 'positive' counterpiece to *The Antichrist*, as Nietzsche's most sustained attempt to free himself from the clutches of negation and 'mere criticism'. Its form consists of a number of parables and oracular pronouncements richly garnished with natural imagery; these are at first organized round a few episodes from the prophet's life, but soon the sequence of story or continuous argument is abandoned. With its oracular phrases and archaicizing turns, the work overtly aspires to being a rival to 'the greatest book in German' – Luther's Bible translation; it often reads like a pastiche of it. Unlike Richard Strauss's *Zarathustra* fantasy, it has no unity of poetic structure to encompass it, relying for its strong effects on lyrical landscape sketches, Blakean vignettes and polished aphorisms.

Its story, such as it is, is soon told. Having 'come down' among men from his mountain solitude, Zarathustra decides to bring them his message; he finds a group in the market-place, watching a tightrope walker perform his act. The man falls – not a devil but his companion has made him lose his balance – and, mortally wounded, is lugged by Zarathustra for a day and a night, and finally buried in the forest. Thereafter we follow Zarathustra, preaching to his disciples, returning again to his solitude, descending for a second and third time . . . A forest, a ship, a mountain meadow and the desert are the settings, and Zarathustra's animals – the lion, the eagle, the snake – his most faithful companions.

Can a myth be deliberately created? A myth without gods, perhaps; but a myth without people? Nietzsche lacks Richard Wagner's sustained mythopoeic gift, and the book is weakest in its presentation of human beings and encounters. Here a comparison with the Bible is most damaging to it. The prophetic or parabolic nature of Christ's sayings does not impair their simple appropriateness to each individual person he addresses, but there is no room for such appropriateness in *Zarathustra*. We hear of Zarathustra's friends and companions, of his deeply felt need for communion with them, but they never arrive. Only his uncomprehending disciples and his enemies – it has escaped the critics' notice how many of the men this 'Yea-sayer to Life' meets are his enemies – make their shadowy appearance on his horrid alp. Though Zarathustra himself is no more than a sublime abstraction,[26] we must not make too much of this literary failure. Once we recognize that Nietzsche has created no person and no genuine dialogue, and that monologue is Zarathustra's main form of discourse, we are free to read the book for what it really is: not a myth at all but the belated descendant of an eighteenth-century philosophical fiction. Its complex and consciously composed form hides *and* reveals that 'spirit of gravity' which represents Nietzsche's crucial 'moral experiment'.

What is Zarathustra's message? He is the prophet of certain ideals of mind and conduct to which Nietzsche gives the collective name 'Superman'. The Superman is open toward the world and its vicissitudes; trusts in others and in chance; in him the cardinal vices of lust, lust for power and egoism are transformed into positive values; and he is in love with the earth, with his own fate, with his own life, and ready to sacrifice that life for . . . life as lived by those who are open toward the world and its vicissitudes; who trust in others and in chance; in whom the cardinal vices . . . Based on the premise of a God-less world, the Superman embodies the enhancement of man's untrammelled will to power under the quasi-religious dispensation of 'the eternal recurrence of the same'. The enemies of Zarathustra and of his message are the frivolous and corrupt 'last men' – the Fellini crew of decadents he first meets in the market-place, the sophisticated modern intellectuals – the 'higher men' whom Nietzsche portrayed in *Beyond Good and Evil*; and 'the underprivileged', 'die Schlechtweggekommenen', whose motives are envy, grudgingness and fear.

A framework of qualifications – phrases like 'not yet' 'for this man only', 'but at this time' – emphasizes the relative character of the values whose advent Zarathustra proclaims, and this relativism determines the dialectic of his parables and maxims. The dialectic is enacted in three stages: 'a→not-a→A'. Here are some examples of it from the first part of the book: the passions and even the conventional values, including love of one's neighbour, are condemned, but they are approved of if they spring, not from deprivation, but from a superabundance of personal being; chastity is commended – to him who finds it easy to practise; prayer is right 'for you but not for me'; war is a valuable test of man *if* its motive is hatred (the emotion of a full heart), not contempt; 'a good war' validates the cause for which it is fought; the gods are condemned, the only god worthy of man's veneration is a graceful, dancing god; justice should be for all men save the judges; you call yourself free, but 'are you one of those who had the right to escape from the yoke? Many there are who threw away their last worth when they threw away their servitude'; and 'many there are that have become too old even for their truths and their victories – a toothless mouth no longer has the right to every truth'. There is (as Thomas Mann observed) more than a touch of Oscar Wilde about many of these formulations.

This dialectic in three stages is the characteristic form of Nietzsche's thinking, not only in *Zarathustra*, but wherever a 're-valuation' is to be undertaken; and that, in a sense, is the aim of all his works from *Human, All-Too-Human* onwards. (1) A *description*, mostly hostile but immensely illuminating, of an accepted value or concept or personal trait forms the first stage (e.g.: pity shames both the pitier and the pitied). (2) There follows a *rejection*, for reasons which are usually surprising and which derive from a projection of the original value beyond its usual range (pity strengthens the weak, destroys the strong; *ergo* destroys 'life'). (3) A *re-interpretation* of the original concept and an eloquent *acceptance* of it in its new form ('true' pity, making the strong aware of their strength, strengthens 'life'). The rhetoric of his descriptions and advocacy is an inseparable aspect of the dialectic – it is this that makes Nietzsche so eminently a literary philosopher.

This dialectic is put in the service of the book's anti-transcendentalist purpose. Again and again Zarathustra calls for an enhancement of man's creativeness in a God-less world whose inhabitants should rejoice in their own mortality. The function of the will to power is to turn chance into intention; to create values and 'make things thinkable', yet not to arrest them in their movement, in their 'process of becoming'; above all to affirm – 'be in love with' – the earth as the source of all living things. For is not man's soul his body? The soul can certainly be nothing that is the body's enemy. Neither death nor suffering demean man, but stasis and that annihilating despair in whose sight all appears senseless and void.

But why, we wonder, is the vocabulary of decline – the 'going down' and 'going under' and the 'shattering' impact of thought and experience – prevalent over the vocabulary of assent? Why do the paeans to the Superman's affirmation of life, too, become so quickly paeans to sacrifice and death? It is as though Nietzsche were afraid to set up too readily and too soon the positive values of graceful ease and harmony and joyful *amor fati*, for no sooner do these values look like being realized in concrete terms than they are rejected as not in the right place after all. It is hard to see where the unqualified positive aspects of the Superman, and of the morality of strenuousness he embodies, might lie. In its negative aspects – its emphasis on self-sacrifice, renunciation of what is agreeable and qualified acceptance of 'ascetic ideals' – this morality is much closer to Christianity than Nietzsche would have us believe; and this has led many writers to see in it the authentic form of Christian morality in our time. Yet it needs no great theological perspicacity to recognize that only a deeply confused age could place its faith in a Christianity without Christ and a Christian morality without redemption.

Nietzsche allows himself no way out of the radical negation. Whatever the will creates is there to be destroyed and overcome: 'Whatever I create and howsoever I love it,' Zarathustra proclaims, 'soon I must be its and my own love's enemy – thus my will commands.' All conquest, including self-overcoming, is for the sake of new, higher values and further conquests of the will to power; and these in turn must be overcome for the sake of yet higher values, a yet greater will to power – to what end?

'The will' – any act of willing – is wholly directed toward the future. Whatever else it may accomplish, it cannot undo what has been done, 'it cannot break time and time's covetousness', unless . . . Is there a condition that makes the will sovereign over the past as well as the future? 'The Riddle and the Vision' [Z III § 2], at once the most moving and the most lurid of Zarathustra's parables, describes that

condition and in doing so places the world of the will
under a metaphysical sanction – a 'theology' of the eternal
return.

A long road, steep and rough with scree, has taken
Zarathustra high into the mountains. A dwarf – the spirit
of gravity – on his shoulder has made his progress difficult,
but now they have come to a gateway and when Zarathustra sits down to rest, the dwarf jumps off his shoulder.
The name inscribed on the gateway, Zarathustra explains
to the dwarf, is 'the Moment'. Here at this gateway, he
continues, the two tracks meet: the one, lasting an
eternity, goes back into the past: the other, another
eternity, leads into the future.

'Do you think, dwarf, that these two tracks contradict
each other, eternally?'

'All that is straight lies,' the dwarf muttered contemptu-
ously. 'All truth is crooked, time itself is a circle.'

'Oh spirit of gravity,' I said angrily, 'do not make things
too easy for yourself. Or I shall leave you here crouching,
lamefoot – was it not I who carried you all this way up?

'Behold this moment!' I continued. 'From this gateway
called the Moment, a long, eternal road leads backwards –
behind us lies an eternity. Must not whatever can run
have run along this road before? Must not whatever can
happen have happened before, have been done before,
have run this way before? And if everything has existed
before, what then do you think of this moment, dwarf?
Must not this gateway too have been here before? And are
not all things so firmly knotted together that this moment
draws all future things after it? And so – itself too? For
whatever can run down this long road must run again.

'And this slow spider which crawls in the moonlight,
and this moonlight itself, and I and you in the gateway,
whispering together, whispering of eternal things – must

we not all have been here before? And must we not come again and run out, along that other road, ahead of us, along that long, ghostly road – must we not eternally come back?'

'. . . und ich und du im Torwege, zusammen flüsternd, von ewigen Dingen flüsternd – müssen wir nicht alle schon dagewesen sein?' It is the high moment of Nietzsche-Zarathustra's vision.

Is it more, though, than a philosopher's dream, the image of his metaphysical 'Sehnsucht'? It is the minimal theology of the age he identified as God-less. To understand the doctrine[27] in the context of Nietzsche's philosophizing is to realize that his serious concern with it arises not from any cosmological speculation, but from his criticism of contemporary ideology. Attacking the fashionable idea of progress, he had argued that 'the goal of humanity' must lie 'in its highest specimens', and these may occur, *and recur*, in every age:[28] the past must contain them, but so must the present and the future. And if we assume that the past stretches backward into infinity, it must contain not only 'the highest specimens' of mankind but *all* of mankind – all that has ever happened and all that can ever happen, including 'the gateway called "the Moment"' where the past ends and the future with *its* infinity begins.[29] *And all meaning* – all truth, value and significance – *must lie in this process* of 'eternal' iteration, or else nowhere at all.

But still we have not explained how the will becomes sovereign over the past. The answer must depend on what value Nietzsche intends to give to his myth: is it to be the source of supreme hope or of total despair? This arbitrariness is irremovable. Looking from the gateway into the future, we see the will reigning supreme: we see the future, and all eternity, undetermined but determinable by our will, and therefore the past too (a replica of the future) wholly determinable by it – the seedbox of hope; looking backward into the past, we find that nothing is determinable, all is determined, including the future, again a replica of the past – a seedbox of black despair.

Supreme hope or total despair? Nothing in between will do. The recurrence is to be absolute, the identity of the indiscernible replicas is to be complete:

> I shall return [Zarathustra proclaims], with this sun, with this earth, with this eagle, with this snake – *not* to a new life, or a better life, or a similar life: . . . I shall return always to this self-same life, in the greatest and in the smallest things, that I may teach again the recurrence of all things . . . that I may speak again the Word of the great noon of the earth and of men, that I may again herald the Superman to all men . . .
> Alas, the man will ever return, the little man will ever return! Once I saw them both naked, the great man and the little man; all too like each other, all too human even the greatest!
> All too little, the greatest! – that was my weariness of men! And eternal recurrence of the smallest too! – that was my weariness with all existence! Alas, disgust . . . [Z III § 13]

The implications of Christian eternity are described → it is rejected → a new conception of eternity is set up: here, once again, is Nietzsche's three-stage dialectic. In extolling 'the earth' and 'the world' as man's only true home, and in calling the body 'man's true soul', Nietzsche at the same time acknowledges and extols man's disposition to transcend himself and his condition, to see himself 'as a transition and a going-under'. But this tendency in man must be given a clear goal, his consciousness – part animal, part metaphysical – must have a clear object: the earth, as the absolute end purpose of man's existence. In other words: the doctrine is designed 'to take the place of metaphysics and religion' [*WP* § 462], *to be* a metaphysics and a religion (it is called an '*eternal recurrence*') but of a negative kind: not to offer consolations for wrongs endured and rewards for virtues practised, but to be a test.

It is not, as some have argued, a contradiction of the idea of the Superman, but the proving of his worth. So powerful is to be his love of life that even when life is perpetuated into infinity in all its greatness and triviality; when these, too, the great and the trivial, come to be seen, devastatingly, as of one kind and then are to be repeated again and again, *ad infinitum* and *ad nauseam*, without change, without improvement, without added meaning or significance . . . if all this, carried on into eternity, is to be the 'meaning' of life, and yet the Superman is to assent to it, give it his active approval and the stamp of his love – then indeed he has proved himself in the most strenuous test which his creator is capable of envisaging, then he has cleansed himself of all false and consoling beliefs, of all spurious comfort and superstition, and is left with a 'faith' that is likely to make all willing, all our vital powers, shrivel up in horror. Then he has exposed himself to the merciless rays of the midday sun, the sun that throws its harsh light into every corner of experience; that leaves no hidden comfort in the dark caves and picturesque grottoes of the old religion.

What Nietzsche is trying to put into words is 'a vision of the world *sub specie aeterni*' – the world as a self-contained, deeply meaningless whole – and this vision I take to be ineffable and thus unassailable. Yet we cannot for long contemplate the image which is designed to express the vision, or think about the concept behind the image, without being struck by its inherent contradictions. Leaving to one side the question of how such a reverence is possible, we may accept it as a metaphysical *donnée* (in the same way as we accept the single occurrence of the world), and confine ourselves to its function as a moral-existential test. The image of 'the great man and the little man' is as moving as it is profound, but what is to make 'the eternal recurrence of it' frightening and nauseous? Repetition entails horror and accidie only if it is accompanied by an awareness of a repeated failure to reach something better, perhaps even some grand metaphysical goal – in any event a good that is outside the world which is to be eternally repeated (for if it were inside the world, it would be part of the repetition). But this involves a destructive contradiction, for the image of the recurrence serves a doctrine which is designed to scotch all thought of anything 'outside' or 'beyond' – any kind of eschatological ideal, of which the Christian ideal is, for Nietzsche, the only conceivable paradigm. We must conclude that, even as a moral-existential test, the doctrine functions only on the premise of a pseudo-Christian eschatology, which is destructive of the purpose for which the doctrine was set up in the first place – the purpose of expressing a vision of the world as a self-contained, deeply meaningless whole. (It does not make the world meaningful, it only makes it not self-contained.) With this kind of dilemma we are familiar from previous arguments. This is the destructive aspect of Nietzsche's three-stage dialectic: each time transcendence is to be rejected for a moral-existential purpose by an authority that bases itself on transcendent grounds.

A vision which aspires to being a doctrine (Nietzsche himself repeatedly calls it '*die Lehre* von der *ewigen*

Wiederkunft'), a theory about the ends of life dictated by an intense personal experience and transfixed into an image, conveying a feeling (to us a deeply familiar feeling) about life, but hardly capable of conceptualization: this is, as Heidegger and others have observed, the culmination of Nietzsche's entire philosophical venture. But since (unlike Heidegger) I have taken Nietzsche's moral-existential concern to be the heart of that venture, I have throughout presented the ontological aspect of Nietzsche's thinking as ancillary. Nietzsche's concern as I see it takes the form of a God-less theology, to which only the *function* of the idea of the eternal recurrence – its value as a moral-existential test – is important.

This 'theology' is Nietzsche's main bequest to the new century. With its heroism of strenuousness, its scepticism of all traditional solutions, its radical rejection of all grace and ease, its occasional pride in despair and its validation through suffering and sacrifice, it became the dominant ideology and 'tablet of values', of Germany at all events, in the era of the two World Wars. It inspired, indeed obsessed, the writings of her greatest literary men and philosophers. From it derives that scrupulousness with which some of these writers (chief among them Thomas Mann) anticipated and tried to oppose those monstrous political solutions whose hallmark was cheapness and brutal simplicity, and which won the day. Yet there is another aspect of this 'heroism of strenuousness': it is also the ground shared by enemies. Reading the literature of national socialism we can no longer ignore the way its rhetoric plays on the need for sacrifice, on the exacting yet self-validating nature of the struggle, on the perils of the road ahead, and on the value of authenticity seen as one man's commitment to his supremely hard (and peferably distasteful) task; and as we follow Hitler's career, too, it becomes evident that its apogee lay, not in the years of his great triumphs, but in those last years of strenuousness when he succeeded in identifying his defective self with a nation and a whole world at war, under the device not of conquest but of destruction.[30] It is no great merit for us to be able to see what neither Nietzsche nor the next generation quite foresaw: that in a situation of lawlessness, with every restraint undermined and 'everything permitted', the idea – accepted as unqualified value – of a validation of man through his own supreme effort, coupled with the allurement of heroic defeat, would lead to horrifying abuse. In estimating the extent of Nietzsche's influence, we must bear in mind that its concrete political consequences were confined to prewar Germany and Italy and, to a lesser extent, war-time France, whereas only its literary and philosophical aspects took root in England. The reason for this is obvious. Men like George Bernard Shaw and H. G. Wells, D. H. Lawrence and W. B. Yeats did not live in a society on the verge of disaffection and anarchy. What prevented them from turning their literary ideas into political realities was the social *donnée* of their lives – an unbroken national tradition of decency and institutionalized freedom, which Nietzsche viewed with little more than contempt.

The morality of strenuousness with its theological overtones does not go uncontradicted in Nietzsche's writings. There are occasions when he attacks it as a distortion of 'the joyful science' about man, as lacking all grace, all love of surfaces and *finesse*. He ridicules the notion that 'strenuous effort in search of truth is supposed to determine the value of that truth', and that ' "truths" are really nothing more than a sort of gymnastic apparatus on which we are supposed to exercise until we are worn out – a morality for athletes and champion gymnasts of the mind.' [*HAH* II § 4] And in the *Zarathustra* chapter entitled 'The Spirit of Gravity' [III § 11] it is precisely the opposite

6 Discontinuities

We have more than once noted the fragmentariness and 'aphoristic' character of Nietzsche's thinking. His impatience with all system and ideology, and his quick contempt for expatiation are the price he must pay for the versatility and liveliness of his philosophical imagination. But can we see beyond the signs of his impatience? Our concern in this chapter is with the essential limitation of Nietzsche's philosophy.

A number of seemingly disconnected observations will point the way. They are all part of a style of thinking in which the category of the single and individual prevails, even where it is irrelevant. Thus Nietzsche's theoretical view of language (to which we shall turn in the last chapter) is atomistic: if meaning and value are to be found anywhere (he argues), it is in the single discrete elements, in metaphors expressive of individual moments of truth. Just as his observations on other men's work tend to be confined to brilliant *aperçus* and single impressions, so the architectonic is the weakest aspect of his own books. Both 'life' and 'the will to power', we recall, were seen as principles relating to the being and morality of individual persons only – on the occasions when the ethos of groups is considered, it is seen as wholly at the mercy of the charismatic leader. Nietzsche's consistent preference is clear: he is always for the single man against the herd, for genius against justice, for grace against deserts; he favours inspiration against the rule of rules and professional competence, and the heroic in every form against all that is 'human, all too human'. His huge and sometimes faulty generalizations are not signs of what Wittgenstein calls 'contempt for the individual case', but signs of an epistemological *amor fati*, that is, of Nietzsche's innermost trust that the single case he cites and generalizes is the exemplary one.

The catastrophic – non-gradual – perception, the unpremeditated insight and sudden conviction, the flash-like inspiration – these, for Nietzsche, are the authentic modes of knowledge-and-experience. And even though, especially in the 'positivist' period of *The Joyful Science* (1882), he praises knowledge which matures slowly and convictions which are deeply considered, the very form in which he does it shows that this is not the way *he* works. He attacks historians for burying great men under a welter of facts, for replacing genuine insights with endless continuities, and for denying that there is genius which does not develop as they develop – slowly, gradually, tediously. 'My way of reporting historical facts', he writes in a note in 1879, 'is really to tell the story of my own experiences *à propos* of past ages and men. *Nothing coherent*: some things became clear to me, others did not. Our literary historians are boring because they force themselves to talk about and pass judgement on everything, even where they have experienced nothing.' [*WKG* IV/3 p. 390] The single experience – '*Erlebnis*' – is all.

There is no end of such reflections, and they all point to a pervasive limitation of Nietzsche's thinking: it is his consistent neglect of, and his indiscriminate bias against, what I shall call *the sphere of association*.

By this I mean that in all his philosophizing he has nothing really positive to say about all those human endeavours – in society, art and religion, in morality, even in the natural sciences – in which single discrete insights and experiences and encounters: single *situations* – are stabilized and made reliable by means of rules and laws and institutions, leading to new associations or combinations, which in turn bring about new situations. Nietzsche, however, sees man's search for stability almost always as an arrest of living experience, an inauthentic pursuit, a fear of the rigours of solitude, a defection from the heroic acceptance of singularity. He seems hardly aware of this process; whenever he does become aware of it, he condemns its results as derivative. Tradition, dogma, formulation itself amount for him to a second order of experience, a spurious, reach-me-down reality. Institutionalization as man's only protection against arbitrariness means little to him. We have seen this bias at work in his wholesale rejection of the Christian Church in the world. If, in *The Antichrist*, he extols Rome as the fountainhead of culture and Imperial stability [§§ 58-9], it is merely to vilify Judaeo-Christian subversiveness. And if, in traditional Romantic fashion, he occasionally disparages 'the State' and glorifies 'the Nation' [Z I § 12], he does so for the simple and predictable reason that he regards the former as the coldest of cold institutional monsters, while in the latter he sees a 'natural' extension of the private self. To enlist him, on the strength of such opinions, either on behalf of the nationalists or of political liberals is equally absurd.

Yet strong political implications follow from this emphasis on '*the sudden*', and on the isolated '*Erlebnis*'. It cannot be denied that this affective rhetoric (rehearsed in numerous metaphors of unbridled violence, strokes of lightning, volcanic eruptions and other such subtleties) was to become central to the ideology of Italian and German fascism and that, with the help of men like Gabriele d'Annunzio and Dietrich Eckart,[1] it would one day be translated from the literary-philosophical sphere into political fantasy, and thence into practical politics. Art above all is, for Nietzsche, the enemy of the hebetude of custom and repetition. Among the reasons why he is so intent on assigning to the aesthetic activity a central role in human existence is his understanding of it as a mode of experience which, more than any other, escapes the sphere of association and lives by the appearance of uniqueness. A good many of his political remarks, including the early essay on 'The Greek State', must be seen in this light: as attempts to heroize the political activity by interpreting it as the highest, Apolline form of aesthetics and by identifying the political leader with the artist in human 'material'. (And when, incidentally but not surprisingly, men like B. Mussolini took their cue from these remarks, they were not misinterpreting them.)

Is it meaningful to make Nietzsche responsible for this development? We must certainly absolve him from responsibility for its last stages. How can lack of prescience be blameworthy? Yet had he discovered a philosopher in a similar predicament, it is unlikely that Nietzsche would have exonerated him, seeing how quick he (Nietzsche) was to equate a failure of the imagination with a moral-existential failure. What it comes to, in the last resort, is that he does not believe in his own beliefs enough to be circumspect about the conditions in which they might one day be realized.

In the dialectic which lies at the core of all human experience Nietzsche always favours the unique against repetition and genius against justice. We may leave to one side for the moment the question whether this is a practicable point of view: what undermines his advocacy and limits his perception is that he does not admit the presence of a genuine dialectic, of an inescapable human problem. Yet although it is inescapable, the problem is of course not insoluble – indeed, all civilized life depends on its on-going solutions. But then, Nietzsche often writes as though this were enough to make civilization itself suspect and by definition decadent.

Whenever social considerations may legitimately be translated into considerations of personal value and dignity, Nietzsche's full critical understanding is brought into play. But there are aspects of social life (such as the law, or politics, or economic exchange) which have a dialectic of their own and to which, therefore, *immediate* personal value judgements are irrelevant. Nietzsche's reflections on these topics show up the bad discontinuity of his thought. My criticism is not that he fails to provide what he never attempted – a systematic sociology – but that the view of society *and* of the individual entailed by his reflections on social morality is flawed.

Characteristically, the only form of government that interests him is rule through a leader's or an oligarchy's absolute exercise of power. But because he does not explore the ways in which even autocratically governed societies are formed and sustained by custom and convention – does not ask how much of the old is bound to survive into the new – he cannot explain rule by command except with the aid of catastrophic 'natural' factors. And since for him, in this context, the 'natural' is an irreducible category [*WP* § 916], the conception of society that emerges from his observations is not that of a self-contained functional system, but a system that works by virtue of its relationship to something outside itself (it is in this sense that the fascist leader claimed to be and indeed was, and the communist leader is, outside politics). Sometimes he sees this outside force as nature, sometimes it is fate, sometimes it is a present god, or again a *deus abscon-*

ditus – yet what Nietzsche intends is the opposite, is a self-contained system of rule. His explicit aim, as we have seen more than once, is to make men self-reliant and self-determining, content with their earthly lot and free from all need of gods, yet the system of social and political life that would be required to institute such an autonomous humanity does not interest him.

Historical change as Nietzsche sees it is brought about by great men who impose their will on the birth-florescence-decay cycles of whole cultures, and these cycles are conceived 'organically', on the analogy of plant life. Between the two poles of individual psychology and cosmic or millennial speculation – between the Superman and the doctrine of 'the eternal recurrence of the same' – there seems to be a void; or rather, not a void, but the curiously unreal picture of a society which is both rigid and provisional, and which (he avers) must be totally transcended.

It is Nietzsche's readiness to follow the fashion of 'social Darwinism' and resort to its 'natural' explanations of a life-and-death struggle – again the analogy with fascist ideologies is at hand – which leads to his conception of society as a thing rigid and unadaptable to gradual change. Instead – and this is what makes the picture so unreal – societies seem to move from complete stability (which he always identifies with oppressive inertia) through sudden catastrophe or authoritarian command to total re-formation: but this, we know, is not how societies change.

Perhaps it is misleading to speak as though Nietzsche presented an actual 'picture' of this or that society, real or utopian – his sketches are never detailed enough for that. What he does is to offer certain moral and ethical exhortations – here is one from each phase of his philosophizing: 'I know of no greater purpose in life than to be destroyed by that which is great and impossible!' [*TS* II § 9]; 'A thousand goals there have been hitherto, for there have been a thousand peoples: only the yoke for the thousand necks is lacking – the one goal!' [Z I § 15]; 'I teach that there are higher men and lower men, and that a single individual can under certain circumstances justify the existence of whole millennia!' [*WP* § 997] – and from such exhortations and invectives he lets us infer the sort of society at which they are directed. Its ethos is always the ethos of the market-place. It is by definition unheroic and inherently decadent.

In addressing the heroic individual man as though such a man stood wholly outside the social nexus, Nietzsche ignores the most important insight of social thought in his age. Early sociologists, among them Marx and Durkheim, but also Max Weber, have shown at length that the individual self, in any living sense, *even as a self* is already implicated in a system of social and moral conventions; that it is nothing without having some relationship to this system; that, as E. H. Carr once put it, Robinson Crusoe is an Englishman and a native of the City of York. The recognition that any act of reform or revolution must be understood in relation to 'the full and explicit realization of the idea of society as a definite circumstance, the main condition of individual life'[2] is to us no less important for being a commonplace, but it is not part of Nietzsche's reflective horizon. He does not quarrel with the central insight of his age: he does not seem to be aware of it. What he attacks as an aspect of the decadence of his world is an essential part of the human condition itself. His consistent rejection of the sphere of association forms the most important and the most disturbing limitation of his philosophical thinking. Moreover, in this attitude he is in no way original, in no way 'the unique event and exception' in the culture of his country. Here he belongs to a dominant German tradition which goes back to Martin Luther and perhaps beyond.

But is it really true to say that Nietzsche does not sufficiently explore the relationship between social convention and the individual's will to power? After all, it is he who not only asserts but shows in convincing detail the 'genealogy of morals' from clerical prohibition and taboos to moral dogmas: in a famous passage in *The Dawn* [§ 9], he argues the '*mores*' origin of morality; elsewhere he describes the source of guilt feelings and the etiology of 'the bad conscience', and points to the sadistic origin of most social and spiritual ideals . . . While we appear to claim that his knowledge of – or at least his interest in – society is inadequate, are we not really proposing a different, rival social morality? If our argument relating to 'the sphere of association' is correct, it follows that Nietzsche's ideas about morality are in an important sense defective and impracticable. Comparison with a more orthodox scheme – less original but more realistic, more like what we know to be the nature of our moral experience – will help us to particularize the defect of his scheme.

In an essay entitled 'Three Strands of Morality', Dorothy Emmet[3] describes the grounds from which moral conduct issues; she calls them 'custom, reciprocity and Grace'. (1) A good many of the decisions we take in the course of our day are made uncritically and without reflection. Life (in no very august meaning of that word) would come to a halt were it not possible to rely on unspoken, unreflected, unchallenged bits of daily conduct, which are yet part of our experience of better and worse, good and evil. Even a self-supporting commune of Californian flower children must either evolve a set of such mores for itself or (this is more likely) transplant them from the society they have repudiated. (2) At any point where these mores are challenged and cease to be 'self-evident' (Miss Emmet writes), 'a reflection on the mixed set of customs which make up [the first] strand' must set in, and the guide of such reflecting will now be a sense of fairness or, at a more comprehensive level, 'reciprocity'. This is the impersonal morality of rules and regulations and laws. (3) And there is finally the morality of Grace 'which is not calculating, however fair and reasonable such calculations may be', but stands 'for the quest of an elusive ideal good which cannot be contained in any set of rules or be expected as of right'. Involving 'a highly personal kind of behaviour', it is 'the morality of saints and heroes', and of humbler people too.

Nietzsche allows no positive value at all to the first, the morality which is ruled by habit and custom. To the extent that he can assimilate habit and custom under the heading of 'instinct', he will emphasize their 'life-enhancing' quality and set them in firm opposition to the second kind of morality, the morality of laws; for the rest he will condemn this morality as inert, unthinking [*HAH* I § 97] and inauthentic [*D* § 455] conformism. '*Dike*', the second kind of morality, he will condemn for its rationalizations, its unheroic protection of 'the weak and under-privileged', its interference with the 'natural' effects of 'the will to power'. It is here, in his attacks on the morality of laws and institutions, that Nietzsche's distrust of everything that makes for stability receives a sympathetic hearing from those protesting minorities in our midst whose survival is assured by the rules of reciprocity they despise.

Nietzsche is therefore left with only one of the three strands, the wholly personal and 'authentic' morality of Grace, which has no rules and follows no precedents and fears no outcome to its generous ventures. This, of course, is to be the morality of the Superman, which flows from a full heart and a clear mind and a love of the earth. However, since for Nietzsche there is no such thing as Grace, we had better speak of a 'morality *as if* from Grace' which, in his scheme, must do duty for all three strands. Not much demonstration is needed to show that life in the world as we know it, governed *solely* by the morality of Grace – which in Nietzsche's utopia turns out to be a single man's fervour – is certain to collapse into anarchy.

Continuity is acknowledged as the essence of every morality [*BGE* § 188], except (it seems) of the scheme that is to emerge from the 're-valuation of all values' (the project which occupied him after 1884). Nietzsche certainly reflects at length on what these new values should be, whether they are to be subsumed under an ethical maxim or whether they are to be part of an aesthetic re-interpretation of the world, and to what new goals they are to lead mankind. But prior to deciding what is to be inscribed on these new 'tablets of values' is the question whether such radically new tablets can be put into practice at all; and to the extent that this is an issue, not of individual psychology, but of the logic of conversion, Nietzsche shows no interest in it. Is it possible for a man to reject one set of values and then decide, with a free mind, on another set? Nietzsche seems to think that a man's freedom of moral choice is unlimited. If every human decision is preceded by a moment of indecision, then a 'decision' in favour of one moral system rather than another is a chimera. No man, other than lunatic or criminal, is ever in a moral vacuum. And if he were, what could possibly cause him to emerge from it? Not the old values, for they are to be rejected (this is to be a radical 're-valuation'), nor yet the new ones, for on these he has not yet decided . . .⁴ Nietzsche's argument lacks a recognition that any new scheme is necessarily continuous with (even: parasitic on) the existent old scheme, and that this state of affairs is not caused by the turpitude of mankind but is inherent in the process of moral reform. Saul (Nietzsche fails to see) was not any Tom, Dick or Harry.

This, then, is Nietzsche's horizon, the limit of one mode of his consciousness. Why can he not think and experiment outside it? Why does he ignore the 'associative' part of our world? The question seems to have a ready answer: because, in a peculiarly radical, German way, he is preoccupied with attacking those currents of contemporary culture and social thought which render his ideal for humanity impossible. At this point the different aspects of the sphere of association fall apart. Nietzsche is reacting against the political ideas of the French Revolution, the social ideas of Rousseau *and* of the English political economists, the nascent international socialist movement and its belief in progress, at the same time as he is reacting against Schopenhauer's and Hegel's expatiations on single themes and against Kant's idealism, which he 'unmasks' as a systematic undermining of man's faith in his senses and in the earth, their object.

However, an answer of this kind is not just obvious, it is also inadequate. His philosophical project cannot be explained in terms of reactions. Its true and irreducible ground is his image of man, 'unhouseled, disappointed, unaneled' and for these reasons heroic, held out into the void of the circle of endless repetitions.

He loves the world, but does not want it to last. His deepest and most consistent concern is not with social values of any kind, neither with the swaggering gilded fuss of the leader nor with the blood-and-iron ideology of the man of will, nor with any of our prudentialisms. The value that is left at the end of his moral arguments is the opposite of any conceivable utopia. It is the heroism of deprivation: a strange 'value', as we have seen, yet part of the discontinuous, catastrophic experience which dominates his outlook and writings. And here (we recall from our earlier comparison with Marx[5]) lies the strongest reason for our feeling that Nietzsche anticipates our world, our familiar landscape of craters and scaffoldings.

7 Aesthetic Re-interpretation

I

Is there no escape from the world of judgement and suffering everlasting? Nietzsche's attempts at an aesthetic validation of existence are intended as a joyful alternative to – a redemption from – the world seen as a manifestation of 'the will to power and nothing else besides'; yet the idea of an enhancement of personal being is not to be abandoned. Selflessness and disinterestedness – attributes of traditional aesthetics – are not available to such a re-interpretation, for they are merely the shamefaced acknowledgements of a small, defective self:

> Since Kant, all talk of art, beauty, knowledge and wisdom is sullied and made messy by the concept of disinterestedness. I regard as beautiful (historically speaking) all that which, in the most revered men of an age, assumes visible shape as the expression of what is *most worthy* of reverence. [*Mus* XVII p. 304]

The peremptory tone reminds us of several other reflections on the borderline between statement of fact and exhortation: we must create men to whom the truth will be useful [*WKG* VII/1 p. 184]; a man's knowledge may not extend beyond his will to power [*BGE* § 211]; his thinking and his action should be one [*Z* I § 5]. All such proposals are indicative of Nietzsche's desire that value should be determined by nothing but the personal being of man, but this desire brings the spectre of solipsism in its train. Nietzsche knows well enough that there is truth which is lethal, knowledge which comes only when

127

the will to power is assuaged, thinking which goes beyond action, and great art which does not express whatever is 'most worthy of reverence'.

Moreover, who *are* 'the most revered men of an age'? Consensus – the opinion of the mob – will not tell us. Are they the men with the superior will to power, those who most joyfully assent to life? The histrionic Wagner is not one of them, nor are 'some of the greatest names in art', including Goethe, for there is 'an actor at the heart of every artist' [*Mus* XVII p. 334], and do not the actor and the comedian represent the sum of spuriousness and in-authenticity [*CW* § 11]? Since Nietzsche is not prepared to consider a work of art as independent of the character of its creator, the aesthetic mode can never be made independent of the moral. From first ('Lest the bow should snap, there is Art,' *TS* IV § 4) to last ('We have Art lest we should perish of the truth,' *WP* § 822) the aesthetic is to be in the service of life – can it also act as a redemption from life? Nietzsche is seeking a corner of the world – but with him it can never be less than a total view of the world – that would be free from all guilt and feeling of guilt: 'It would be terrible if we still believed in sin: no, whatever we shall do, in countless repetitions, it will be *innocent*. There is no guilt if the thought of the eternal recurrence does not overwhelm you, no merit if it does.' [*WKG* V/2 p. 394] Well then – since 'God is dead' and we no longer believe in sin, has not the reign of innocence come? Even in his most euphoric moments Nietzsche does not believe this. Once again, therefore, he moves from statement of fact to exhortation: if 'God is dead', the artist will be god and Nietzsche will proclaim his theodicy:

> Only as an aesthetic phenomenon is the world and the existence of man eternally justified.

We recall this strange sentence from *The Birth of Tragedy* (see above, p. 48), where it seemed disconnected from the contexts in which it appeared. But since it was written down at least fifteen years before 'the death of God' was announced for the first time, is there any indication that this experience casts its shadow over Nietzsche's first book too? Certainly there is no explicit mention of this anguished, wholly modern recognition, yet the quasi-religious strain (to which Nietzsche draws attention in his preface to the 1886 edition) is certainly present, nowhere more so than in that disconnected sentence: in the word 'eternal', in the absoluteness – '*only* as . . .' – of the claim, and in the 'justification', the God-less theodicy. Man's judging activity is not repudiated (as it will be in *Antichrist*, Nietzsche's last completed work), but it is to be conducted from a different, all-encompassing point of view. In the high noon of Nietzsche's thinking the entire world and all that we do in it is seen as a sort of game or play, a spectacle for the gods if there are any gods to watch it:

> Around the hero everything turns into tragedy, around the demi-god everything turns into satyric drama; and around God everything turns into – what? Maybe the 'world'? [*BGE* § 150]

The world's gravity and seriousness – its tragic dimension – is rendered weightless (as time is rendered endless in the idea of the 'eternal' recurrence) – weightless, yet infinitely more memorable than it had ever been in its aesthetically unredeemed state. Only in this form does the world become what Nietzsche wants it to be: the worthy object of a limitless, total affirmation. And in this idea of an aesthetic theodicy the eternal recurrence too, seen as an unending game or spectacle [*WP* §§ 1066-7], receives its final 'justification'.

Nietzsche loved the image of the snake: the beginning and the end of his philosophizing close in a circle. The tragic divinity at the centre of his first book is taken up again in the panegyrics to Dionysian creativeness at the end of *Beyond Good and Evil* and in the last notes to *The Will to Power*. It is in these notes that the unconditioned assent to the single moment of happiness is identified with Dionysus, the god of chaos, fertility and the enhancement of life through the threat of death [§ 1032], and the world is celebrated as a dancing god, or again as a child. Here [§ 1039] Nietzsche at last records the self-destructive truth that only those who are possessed by the spirit of gravity ever yearn for the ideals of lightness and grace, and go out in search of them. Dionysus now becomes the name of that divinity which, transcending any narrowly aesthetic idea, transforms and 'eternally justifies' the world of suffering; the Dionysian is that tragic mode of being and view of life whose source is not weakness and decadence but 'an excess of force' and vitality [*TI* X § 4]; Dionysus now seems to stand for all creation, everything . . . But does it matter by what name that limitless affirmation is to be called?

It does matter. As long as Nietzsche calls his ideal of affirmation 'Dionysus', he is still involved in the world of conflict and strife. Dionysus still acts as a judge of men, shaming us in our velleities and deprivations [*WP* § 1051]. While he has an antagonist, the assent he commands cannot be total. And indeed, as Nietzsche tells us in these late notes, written in the summer of 1888, there is a rival deity. Its name is no longer Apollo (the Apolline is now subsumed under the Dionysian), but Christ. But is Dionysus as Nietzsche sees him really Christ's antagonist? Intuitively aware of the close tie between the one whom the Maenads tore limb from limb and the one who was crucified, the poet Hölderlin had united both in a single elegiac vision. Nietzsche thrusts them apart:

> Dionysus versus 'the Crucified': there you have the antithesis. The difference is not in respect of their martyrdom but of its meaning. Life itself, its eternal fruitfulness and recurrence, involves torment, destruction, the will to annihilation. In the other case suffering – 'the Crucified as the innocent one' – serves as an argument against this life and as a formula for its condemnation. Evidently, what is at issue is the problem of the meaning – Christian or tragic? – of suffering. In the former case it is to be the way toward holy being, in the latter, being itself is holy enough to justify an enormity of suffering . . . The god on the cross is a curse on life, pointing to a redemption from life: Dionysus torn to pieces is a promise of life – it will be eternally reborn and return again from destruction. [*WP* § 1052]

We can see why Nietzsche, the declared enemy of Christian eschatology, wishes to widen the gulf between his two deities. And yet: there can hardly be anything more Christian, anything closer to the mystery of the man-and-God on the cross, than Nietzsche's Dionysian justification of the world, of which he says that it transfigures the world's suffering without robbing it of its reality; and there can hardly be anything less 'aesthetic'.

Is there then no end to the conflict, no end to judging? If the god Dionysus does not vouchsafe it, what will? In one of the chapters he wrote (1873) for his unfinished *Philosophy in the Tragic Age of the Greeks*, Nietzsche had meditated on Heraclitus's apophthegm, 'The Aeon [=time] is a child, playing draughts; a child's is the kingdom', which Heidegger interprets, 'Being within the Whole is governed by innocence'. This is certainly Nietzsche's meaning: freedom from guilt and responsibility –

the end of all judging – but also freedom from the burden of consciousness, shall mark the child's dominion over 'the Kingdom', over 'Being within the Whole'. To this liberating conception Nietzsche returns in the first of Zarathustra's parables[1] and in a note (as fragmentary as any of Heraclitus's) in *The Will to Power*, dated 1885/6 [§ 797]. Reflecting on a childlike divinity of supreme innocence whose 'play' comprises – perhaps *is* – 'the Kingdom', Nietzsche is offering the image of the child as an 'aesthetic justification', not only beyond good and evil, but beyond all conflict, all antagonisms. We can make little of the few words on the page.[2] The intimation is too brief, the air too thin to carry the argument. Among Nietzsche's many inconclusive conclusions, this vision of the world justified in its totality as a child's play, characterizes his deepest yearning yet remains the least conclusive and the least convincing. Conflict and lethal strife are inseparable from his reflections on the world, even from those euphoric jottings with which he leaves it and enters the night of madness. And since this conflict to the last is a sign of his truthfulness, victory is not with 'the aesthetic'. Dionysus is the name he signs on his last notes; *and* 'The Crucified'. 'Here you have the antithesis.'

II

One more task remains: to consider the question how to read Nietzsche's writings, how to understand the mode in which they are cast.

In 1873 (a year after *The Birth of Tragedy*) Nietzsche dictated to his old schoolfriend, Carl von Gersdorff, an essay entitled 'On Truth and Falsehood in an Extra-Moral Sense'.[3] Although this is only a short essay of fifteen pages, hardly corrected by Nietzsche and not published until

1903, it is probably the longest single essay on a traditional 'philosophical' subject he ever composed. It is an imperfect piece, and we shall have to supplement its argument from Nietzsche's contemporary notebooks and later reflections, but it contains his only considered statement on the nature and metaphysics of language.

At its centre is the claim that language, far from giving us a true account of things as they are in the world, and far from having its grounds in 'true reality', is a referentially unreliable set of *almost* entirely arbitrary signs, made up by us in order to safeguard life and the species. Whereas we like to think that the value of language is commensurate with the amount of truth about the world it secures for us, its real value to us is merely a pragmatic one, to do with whether or not it works. Its principal function is to hide from us the hostile nature of the universe in order to preserve us from destruction – at least for a little while; therefore the lie about what the universe is really like is not a contingent aspect of language, but its very essence. The falsehood of language in an 'extra-moral sense' (as the title of the essay puts it) consists in the vital pretence that language is able to relate the world of men to some wider, benevolent cosmic scheme by offering them reliable knowledge of that scheme, whereas the universe can get on perfectly well without the world of men and is merely waiting for an opportunity to continue on its desolate journey through man-less aeons. The 'moral' sense of lying, on the other hand, is confined to violating the linguistic, lexical or semantic conventions we have set up in order to get on with each other as best we may. No knowledge of a world beyond our world is available to us. All statements pretending to such knowledge are false, whereas all statements claiming to be *true* accounts of our world are mere tautology:

If someone hides a thing behind a bush, looks for it there and indeed finds it, then such searching and finding is nothing very praiseworthy: but that precisely is what the searching and finding of 'truth' within the realm of reason amounts to.

How then (Nietzsche asks)[4], if we have no positive contact with 'the real world', can we sustain life? How is it that the world works? It works with the help of an illusion, on an 'as if –' principle. We act in the world as if we were in touch with a benevolent reality, as if we were capable of comprehending its cosmic purpose, as if there were a divinity whose decrees we fulfil and that gives meaning to our individual lives.

Between words and things there is no direct relationship (things are not simply the causes of words), and yet the two are not completely unrelated: words are said to be the distant and distorted 'echoes of nervous impulses'. These 'echoes' or rudimentary elements are 'poeticized' and given coherence according to rules entirely invented by man: the relationship that obtains between words and 'the real world' is a metaphorical or aesthetic one. Man as the Idealist philosophers saw him – man as the unstable, contingent perceiving subject of an objective world – is re-interpreted in Nietzsche's scheme as man the creator of language. The relationship which obtains between subject and object – between human language and the real things in the world from which language is excluded – is not a causal relationship for between two such heterogeneous things as subject and object no direct relationship can exist. Nor is it mimetic or expressive, but what Nietzsche calls 'at most an aesthetic attitude',

. . . by which I mean an intimatory transference, a sort of halting, stammering translation into an entirely foreign language: for which purpose we need a freely poeticizing, a freely inventive middle sphere and middle faculty.

This 'poeticizing translation into an entirely foreign language' Nietzsche now likens to the production of Chladny's figures, which are obtained by playing the bow of a violin against a board of thin plywood covered with fine sand; the regular geometrical patterns into which the grains of sand arrange themselves thus reflect or reproduce the vibrations of the music. These figures are as it were metaphorical representations of the music – metaphors of a metaphor. Though it might not be absurd to claim that you can tell from these patterns what it is that men mean by the word 'tone', the patterns will certainly not tell you anything about the nature and meaning of music.

This picturesque yet accurate image aptly illustrates Nietzsche's historical situation. We note his predilection for an analogy drawn from the realm of the natural sciences such as was fashionable in the heyday of the scientific ideology: it seems that all we need do to explain the mental operation involved in the creation of language is to translate the mechanical causality of Chladny's figures into the sphere of mind. Many of the psychological reflections in the books of Nietzsche's most mature period – especially in *Beyond Good and Evil* and its sequel, *The Genealogy of Morals* – are founded in analogies which involve just such a psycho-physical causality, so that it looks as though Nietzsche was on the point of accepting one of the mechanistic and materialistic psychologies current at the time. *Almost* the opposite is the case. By pointing to Chladny's sound patterns, and to the fact that whatever else they do, they do not explain the meaning of music, Nietzsche is in fact showing how inadequate the analogy – the argument from the Chladny figures –

really is, and thus pointing to the break between the psychic and the physical, between mechanical purpose and human meaning.

The way Nietzsche chooses to describe the system sketched out in this essay (and we recall that he started life as a classical philologist) is by saying that words do not designate things and are not little labels stuck on to things, but are *metaphors* for real things in the world:

> What then is truth? A mobile army of metaphors, metonymics, anthropomorphisms – in short, a sum of human relations which, poetically and rhetorically intensified, became transposed and adorned, and which after long usage by a people seem fixd, canonical and binding on them. Truths are illusions which one has forgotten *are* illusions.

– and if, so far, the passage was cast in the form of a fairly neutral philosophical hypothesis, now the point has been reached where Nietzsche can no longer let go without thrusting a value-judgement over the whole argument –

> Truths are illusions which one has forgotten *are* illusions, worn-out metaphors which have become powerless to affect the sense, coins which have their obverse effaced and are now no longer of account as coins but merely as metal.

There is no need to emphasize the powerful imagination at work in this metaphorical account of the nature of metaphors, an imagination that points to and intimates rather than sets out to prove its insights. What the statement reveals is fundamental to Nietzsche's literary practice and therefore to the way in which we must read his writings. If 'Truths . . . are metaphors', then truth (such

as we are capable of conceiving) is in metaphor only : this
'linguistic' insight is the stylistic correlative of Nietzsche's
'experimental' thinking. It enters the many styles Nietzsche
acknowledged as his own at the most intimate and
instinctive level of his writing; sometimes (as in his
excessive use of '*as*' analogies) to its detriment.

Neither in this essay nor anywhere else does Nietzsche
offer a radical criticism of the language of universal and
metaphysical concepts (in the way that e.g. Wittgenstein
does). He sanctions generalizations and conceptual statements of every kind – metaphysical or empirical – as a
part of that complex system of linguistic conventions by
means of which men are enabled to live in the world.
Concepts (Nietzsche writes in the concluding section) are
not fundamentally different from other parts of our
language. He likens them to dice – 'they are made of hard
bone . . . octangular and negotiable, like dice . . .; but even
as such they are the residue of metaphors', that is, of
'nervous impulses' translated into particular names.[5] When
Nietzsche likens concepts to coin (money), he illuminates
their nature in much the same way as the young Marx
had illuminated the nature of money (coin) by likening
it to concepts and thus identifying the function of coin
as that of a mediator between men and the goods they
would have, their '*demande*'.[6] But whereas Marx's ultimate aim is to unmask the metaphorical shift and subject
it to a radical criticism, Nietzsche accepts it as part of 'the
lie' and thus as the *donnée* of our situation in the world.
Concepts are no more – but also no less – than convenient
because life-sustaining fictions. This is the first move in
an argument which ten years later produces the definition of 'the supreme will to power' as a man's determination 'to impose on "becoming" the character of
"Being" ' [*WP* § 617], and by the end of 1888 makes of
all Being 'an empty fiction. The "apparent" world is the

only one there is; the "true" world has merely been mendaciously added.' [*TI* III § 2] And the lie is ineradicable: language (we recall the passage from *The Antichrist*, see above, p. 100) is 'fixed, all that is fixed kills'. It cannot adequately express 'becoming', which is the very nature of our existence [*WP* § 715].

What are we to make of that strange, idiosyncratic insistence on the 'lying' nature of language? Why does Nietzsche refuse to distinguish between 'fictions' and 'lies'? Plato (in the tenth book of the *Republic*) ignores the distinction because by branding fiction as a lie he hopes to safeguard the *polis* from the effects of poetic irresponsibility. Nietzsche on the other hand cares little for the *polis*; 'life', not the *polis* nor even 'the world', is the real object of his concern. 'Life' is never a concept but a vision, a metaphor which embraces all kinds of being but is devalued when it is seen unheroically, under the aspect of association. Yet for us who live in the world it is obvious to the point of banality that there *is* a difference between myth or fiction or poetry on the one hand and the lie on the other, and that this difference derives its entire meaning from an organized legal or moral and therefore social context – from the sphere of association. Only to one who is prepared to take institutionalized life in the world seriously is this difference of any consequence; *sub specie aeterni*, in terms of an aesthetic justification, it disappears. Nietzsche leaves it unexplored.

We can never speak of 'fiction', 'myth' or 'lies' without implying some kind of truth. And Nietzsche, too, claiming that 'truth, *for us*, is no more' than the agreement to play a game of dice in a certain way, implies that there must be something other, something more . . . : but he leaves the space occupied by that other thing empty. It is as if his formulations were deliberately open-ended, as if he delighted in teasing out their implications and then ignoring them.

The aesthetic (we saw in the first part of this chapter) is at odds with the truth about the world. Language (we may now add), being merely 'a mobile army of metaphors', is seen predominantly as an aesthetic phenomenon; and from this two important conclusions follow.

First, the activity of artists – traditionally seen as the makers of metaphors – and the aesthetic activity in general assume an entirely central position in the world. Art is in no sense esoteric or marginal, but becomes the human activity *par excellence*: it is creative existence. The 'justification' of the world through 'the aesthetic activity' is identical with the 'justification' or meaning imprinted on the world through man the maker of linguistic conventions, that is, of a system of 'metaphors'. This in turn implies that gnosis on which Nietzsche's theory of tragedy was founded: it implies the existence of a hostile universe of silence before and beyond language, within which our little human world of language is an oasis of life, comfort and sustenance, but not of *truth*.

Secondly, to see language as an army of metaphors is to see it as a system of signs which, unlike other such systems, is tied to an historical dimension. Its changing nature is built into this scheme by means of its very formulations:[7] he speaks of the 'long usage' in the course of which words become 'fixed, canonical and binding' on a people; metaphors become 'hard' and 'rigid'; or again they wear out and 'lose their sensuous power'; images are effaced and cease to be valid . . . In all this there is change, movement, a course of history, but it is a process which runs all one way, from pristine freshness to ossification, decadence, and an apocalyptic ending. The linguistic process of cliché-formation (which is what the 'petrifaction of words' amounts to) confirms Nietzsche's powerfully negative evaluation of each subsequent stage of European history from the age of Classical Greece onwards, just as it confirms his quasi-Pietist rejection of Christian dogma and doctrine.

'Being', we recall, is the lie imposed on 'becoming'. Words make no sense unless they are arranged in a way that makes them 'fixed, canonical and binding', yet once they are so arranged, they cease to communicate with 'life'. The regularization of the elements of language is condemned because it too (Nietzsche believes) proceeds from 'the lie' at the heart of the language-'reality' relationship. Our criticism of Nietzsche's linguistic views merges with our criticism of his moral and religious reflections: language too belongs to that sphere of association which for him is the sphere of the derivative and inauthentic because he shares that strange (German and Lutheran?) superstition which values origins and singularities more highly than continuities and collectives, and sees every structure as a betrayal of the elements that compose it.[8]

The reflection and the aphorism as units of literary expression, the bright idea as the unit of philosophical thinking, the anecdote[9] as the unit of biography and history, the moment and the single mood – these are the lodestars that guide Nietzsche's venture. With the poet Rainer Maria Rilke he shares 'that dark premonition that this would be life: full of single, particular things, which are made for each man only, and which cannot be *said*.' But it is not only a dark premonition. Those 'moments of assent to all Being' [*WP* § 32], too, are part of his venture, and to them he owes that 'light- and colour-scale of Dionysian happiness' [*WP* § 1051] which Rilke celebrates in the Ninth Duino Elegy:[10]

Ein *Mal*

jedes, nur ein Mal. Ein Mal und nicht mehr. Und wir auch ein Mal. Nie wieder.

Once

Each thing but *once*. *Once* and no more. And we also are *once*. Never again.

III

Nietzsche does not contribute significantly to twentieth-century linguistic thinking because he does not anticipate the discoveries on which it is founded. Among these is Saussure's[11] view of language as a self-contained system or structure. Nietzsche thinks that he has disposed of the truth-value of language by calling its arrangements a mere convention (a structure or system). He argues throughout on the assumption that the elements of language receive their particular meanings from the contexts in which they occur, yet he ignores the fact that any system or structure is more than its parts; that by virtue of being what it is, a structure imposes stability upon its constitutive elements; and that these elements are defined by their relations within the structure. (In just this way he ignored the positive aspects of the rule of custom and law, and every moral or religious institution which related single insights and truths to each other, and thus stabilized them.) Perhaps he takes some parts of this argument for granted. He is not interested in language for its own sake but in its relationship with all that seems to lie beyond it. Is he then saying that a non-linguistic, non-metaphorical numinous world exists after all? Sometimes it seems to enter Nietzsche's argument inadvertently (as when he complains that language is 'not an *adequate* expression' for . . . what realities?); at other times the existence of such an ineffable world is irresistibly implied (in such words as '*meta*phor' and '*translation*', or again in Nietzsche's insistence that something – 'mere metal' – is left over once the inscription of the coin has been rubbed off by wear). He uses every occasion to attack the idea of such a world as a Platonist-Christian-Idealist swindle, yet he never finally relinquishes it either. His linguistic observations must be seen as a foreground argument. Behind them he postulates a non-metaphorical, 'true' order of things to which language does not belong but to which it is somehow related – 'aesthetically', by way of a 'halting, stammering *r*eproduction of . . .' we cannot say what. And this, precisely, is the linguistic analogy to the idea of a social system that works by virtue of its relationship to something outside itself.

That there is a numinous (though destructive) order of things to which language does not belong was the metaphysical claim on which *The Birth of Tragedy* was founded. The anti-Socratic attitude, central to that book, culminated in an attack on language-dominated cultures. There is hardly a book of Nietzsche's in which the value and 'authenticity' of language are not slighted: 'Whatever we have words for, we have already outgrown. In all talk there is a grain of contempt. Language, it seems, has been invented only for the average, for the middling and communicable. Language vulgarizes the speaker.' [*TI* IX § 26]

How then should he convey his vision of the metaphysics of language, Zarathustra's conviction that 'man is a rope, tied between animal and Superman', and that 'what may be loved in man is that he is a transition'? There is no direct way of doing it, yet Nietzsche's passion for *writing* – the obverse of the enticement of insanity and of the fear of silence – remains with him to the end:

to resolve this dilemma he devises his characteristic style of indirection and metaphors.

Where does this style find its vocabulary, how is it assembled? The essay of 1873 ends with a description of the creative intellect that has freed itself from all practical considerations and tasks and sets out, disinterestedly, to re-enact the world in images and concepts. So far the young Nietzsche's argument is pure Schopenhauer. But when Nietzsche goes on to show how this creative mind in its freedom takes up both the vocabulary of common discourse and the scaffolding of concepts 'in order to dismantle them, break up their order and reconstitute them ironically, bringing together things farthest apart and separating those closest together', for no other purpose than to play with them; and when he concludes that

. . . no regular way leads from such intuitions to the land of ghostly abstractions, it is not for them that the word was created; seeing them, man falls silent or speaks in forbidden metaphors and extravagant combinations of concepts, so that by demolishing and by mocking the old conceptual boundaries (if in no other way) he may show himself equal to the impression with which the mighty intuition seized him

— Nietzsche is giving us the most accurate description we have of his own future philosophical and literary procedure.[12]

What that image of the artist at work among forbidden metaphors and untoward combinations of concepts suggests is the act of writing as demolition and de-construction: the breaking up of accepted order is manifest in the pointed brevity of each utterance. And with this goes Nietzsche's discovery that his discrete reflections have value and make sense, that discontinuity can be significant, that 'notes for' a philosophy *are* a philosophy. (Bertolt Brecht, Anton von Webern, Beckett and Borges, Picasso and Braque, made similar discoveries in *their* media.) In just this way Nietzsche will 'bring together and separate' the elements of those cardinal metaphors for which his writings are famous: '*amor fati*', invoking choice motivated by love where blind fate is sovereign; 'the aesthetic justification' where there is to be no 'justifying' or judging; 'the lie in a supra-moral sense'; 'the eternal recurrence' where 'eternity' is to be merely hideous endlessness; 'the death of God' which does not tell us whether he was ever alive; and 'the will to power' which is forever destroying its products and itself – all examples of a metaphysics of which the least confusing thing to say is that it consistently avoids the dangers of dogma and petrifaction at the price of being consistently paradoxical.

There are critics of Nietzsche who have read his work as that of a traditional nineteenth-century German conceptual philosopher or ideologist who, from irresponsibility, demagogy, or sheer ineptitude, made things unnecessarily easy for himself and unnecessarily difficult for his readers by indulging in metaphor-mindedness. Critics of this sort see it as their task to demythologize Nietzsche's writings and, having freed them from their metaphors, to consider how much – or rather how little – remains valid in terms of a conceptually legitimized scheme or system. Others have taken the opposite view: they have seen him as a poet – either as a heroic poet of the German soul (in a tradition that goes from Hölderlin to Rilke, Stefan George and Paul Celan), or as a pre-fascist poet manqué with a penchant for *art nouveau* heraldic beasts and a permanent place in Pseud's Corner. The present essay is written in the belief that this alternative, poet *versus* philosopher, is misleading.

What Nietzsche has evolved in those sixteen years he was granted for his philosophical venture is a variety of styles which are metaphorical in the sense outlined in that early essay of his and in the later observations that spring from it. It is a mode of writing somewhere between the individuation and concern with particulars which is the language area of *belles-lettres*, and conceptual generalities and abstractions which make up the language area of traditional Kantian and post-Kantian philosophy. When Nietzsche refers to the image of the silver coin with its effaced inscription, its value reduced to that of the metal alone, he has in mind neither the coin itself (he is not telling a story), nor a generality which would make the actual image of the coin merely an illustration and therefore dispensable. The metaphor of the coin is intended as an intermediary between two modes of thinking and writing, as a pattern which determines neither a narrative line nor a piece of philosophical poetry or 'Begriffsdichtung', but a philosophical argument.

This middle mode of discourse can certainly be *shown* (and to show it has been the purpose of this chapter), but I am not clear how it can be defined more precisely. It is not poetry: Nietzsche's poetry is less distinguished and less important than his prose. Nor is it poetic prose— the poetic prose he wrote is only rarely successful, in parts of *Zarathustra* it is (in itself and in its influence) a disaster. Nor is it aphorism—Nietzsche's strictly aphoristic utterances are less interesting than those of La Rochefoucauld and Lichtenberg, the two practitioners of the genre whom he most admired. And it is certainly not the conceptual language of philosophy: on the occasion when, in his treatment of traditional philosophical problems (e.g. in his polemics against Kant), he uses such a language, his style becomes impatient, repetitious and often perfunctory. The true distinction of his work, and the true ground of his immensely wide and often over-powering influence, lies in this middle mode of language, which I suppose we may call 'literary-philosophical'; to have devised this mode and applied it to an almost infinite variety of contemporary issues is his greatest achievement. Yet from this mode too springs that entirely modern (and depressingly familiar) habit of talking metaphorically about 'God', 'saintliness', 'divine creation', 'sin' and the like without ever quite deciding what non-metaphorical meanings, and what beliefs (if any), go with the talking.

The disdain with which he treated the sphere of association and the consequent limitations of his view of life in the world have been mentioned, but there is another, positive side to this story. The guiding intention of his philosophical prose is to convey not the general or the average but the unique; to preserve the dynamic, unsteady, the irregular and above all the individualized nature of life. He fears being 'formulated, sprawling on a pin'. His aim is to let the process of 'becoming' speak, to remove the description of 'life' as little as possible from its uncertain, catastrophic origins and destination, even at the price of intellectual coherence itself. Language, metaphor and thought are related to 'the real world' as patterns and paradigms of our being in *its* relationship to 'the real world': there is no such thing as 'Being at rest with itself, identical with itself, unaltering: the only "Being" vouchsafed to us is changing, not identical with itself, it is involved in relationships' . . . [*WKG* V/2 p. 468]

8 Conclusion

Being involved in relationships: the ever-renewed attempts to preserve these 'relationships' from petrifaction fill Nietzsche's books and notebooks, this is what he sees as the task of his philosophical *and* literary undertaking. It is not surprising that Nietzsche's hybrid mode of writing is forever in danger of being impatiently dismissed as 'neither one thing nor t'other', for it constitutes a provocation of the genre theories and tacit assumptions on which French and English kinds of discourse are founded. But it has its antecedents (great writers are hardly ever formal innovators) in Proverbs and in what remains of the writings of the pre-Socratics, in Pascal and a number of German Romantics as well as a few English writers like William Blake; and it has a succession, the language of 'family likenesses', 'blurred photographs', and metaphors of games of Wittgenstein's *Philosophical Investigations*.

What Nietzsche teaches us is not to read philosophy as literature, let alone literature as philosophy, but to read both as closely related forms of life. In challenging, through his mode of writing, the dichotomy of 'scientific' *versus* 'imaginative', or again the antithesis between 'concept' and 'metaphor', 'abstract' and 'concrete', he is at the same time intent on challenging those divisions in our areas of knowledge-and-experience and that fragmentation of knowledge which he (together with other nineteenth-century thinkers, men like Marx, Carlyle and Matthew Arnold) saw as one of the chief blights of modern Western civilization.

Was Heidegger right when he declared that Nietzsche's

work was *finis metaphysicae*? In Nietzsche's philosophizing, and through its very form, a series of traditional metaphysical topics is challenged and rendered problematic. Yet in spite of the form in which they appear, these topics are never wholly refuted; they remain implied in the terminology of the refutations. Nietzsche's ultimate intention was not to destroy metaphysics but to create a new, more timely system. In that, as in all his extended projects, he failed – I think we may say, fortunately. There is no Nietzschean revolution, but there is a new way of looking at the world – his world and ours – and a new style of describing it. And yet he is 'a modern master': no description undertaken with any intensity leaves things as they are, least of all Nietzsche's.

If I spoke of the failure of Nietzsche's attempts at an aesthetic justification of the world, what I had in mind is not only his inability to offer an aesthetic 'system' as an alternative to a moral one; his distrust of system, one of his virtues as a thinker, is too deep for that. But there is also his practice of judging, a part of his Protestant morality. It is too deeply ingrained to allow more than glimpses of alternative ways of responding to the world: hence his inability to show with any richness of detail comparable with the richness of the scenes he presents from the moral world, what this other 'world and being of man' beyond good and evil might be like.

No man's freedom from the restraints of his time and place is absolute; the project of a total self-creation of values is chimeric. (What is not chimeric is the destruction of accepted values which such a project entails, and in this the totalitarian ideologists were only too willing to take his experiments for precepts.) Nietzsche's superb understanding of the spirit of classical Greece does not make him into a Greek thinker. His rejections of every aspect of Christian dogma and faith still leave him an apostate Christian.

Where then does he succeed? His failures are also his success. He understands and 'unmasks' the ethic of blame and praise, punishment and reward, and of the agony of conscience, better than any other thinker. Respecting the variety of life more than he respects the variety of men, he shows what it means to approach each moral-existential issue with a fresh mind; what it means to philosophize against the greatest intellectual and personal odds a man can devise; and what it means to philosophize in an age without a living faith, 'at the torpid turn of the world'. For these purposes he fashions, not a whole new language (which would be as absurd as the project for totally new values), but a new style of understanding, and therefore also participating, in his world and ours. That 'God is dead', that the world is the product of the will to power, and that true value lies in a morality of strenuousness are Nietzsche's formulations for convictions on which much of our lives is based. They are not (I believe) true convictions. Yet no man has been more imaginative in trying to see what the world would be like if they were true.

More than the work of any other philosopher, Nietzsche's work is experiment and hypothesis, not precept. This means that any valid criticism of it must concern itself with the question of how to read him. Best, perhaps, as we read the turbulent late autumn sky with its dramatic greens and melancholy blue-greys and lurid streaks of vermilion; its broken towers and crenellations, its wild riders and other shapes, too, 'like a camel . . . very like a whale' : to read him for the signs of today and tomorrow. But signs of such intensity must always be more than signs.

Notes

Details of books mentioned in the Short Bibliography are not repeated here.

1 Nietzsche in Company

1 See *Die Philosophie im tragischen Zeitalter der Griechen* § 5 (1873).
2 Bertolt Brecht, *Kleines Organon für das Theater* (1953) § 75.
3 See the 1899 testament of Theodor Mommsen, Germany's greatest Roman historian, in Alfred Heuss, *T.M. und das neunzehnte Jahrhundert* (Kiel 1956), pp. 282 f.
4 See John Berger's brilliant comparison of Herzen and Marx, in *Selected Essays and Articles* (Harmondsworth, Penguin paperback, 1972), p. 85.

2 A Chronology of Nietzsche's Life

1 Or possibly Wilhelm Bismarck, the Chancellor's eldest son, who was a rabid anti-Semite.

5 Three Moral Experiments

1 I take this term, together with much else, from Karl Jaspers's work: *N: Einführung in das Verständnis seines Philosophierens*. This is one of the earliest and most distinguished studies of N.

2 This, too, is the concern of Goethe's *Faust*, where Nietzsche found the term 'Übermensch'.

3 W. Kaufmann, *N: Philosopher, Psychologist, Antichrist*, p. 149.

4 To Overbeck, 23 June 1881.

5 See, e.g., *WKG* VII/2 p. 142, *BGE* § 11: 'die Perspectiven-Optik des Lebens'; *JS* V § 374.

6 *JS* III § 270; cf. also *Z* IV § 1 and the subtitle of *EH*, 'How one becomes what one is'. N first mentions the Pindaric apophthegm in a letter to Rohde, 3 November 1867; cf. also Kaufmann, *op. cit.*, p. 159n.

7 See Bernard Williams, *Morality: an Introduction to Ethics* (Harmondsworth 1973), p. 97.

8 See Lionel Trilling's last essay, *Sincerity and Authenticity* (London 1972).

9 15 February 1766, see J. Boswell's *Life of Johnson* (Everyman edn, London 1938) vol. I, p. 318; my italics.

10 See 'The Will to Power in Nature', a chapter in the posthumous compilation comprising *WP* §§ 618-715 (ed. Kaufmann, pp. 332-81); it contains amateurish references to contemporary physics and biology.

11 But this is contradicted by N in *Mus* XIV p. 58.

12 Kaufmann, *op. cit.*, pp. 200, 248, etc.

13 See Eugen Fink's excellent study, *N's Philosophie*, pp. 127 f; see especially *WKG* VII/2 p. 179, quoted above, p. 60.

14 See *Die Welt als Wille und Vorstellung*, vol. I, § 18.

15 Kaufmann, *loc. cit.*, p. 248.

16 See *WKG* VII/3 p. 376, quoted above, p. 20; see also Jaspers, *op. cit.*, pp. 297-8.

17 N's high pedagogic vision mercifully hides from his view the serviettes and elastic braces with the Master's pictures on them, which were being sold in the streets of this new musical academe of the German spirit.

18 'terrible news': *WKG* VII/3 pp. 144 f.; 'loneliness': *ibid* p. 213, both written in 1885; 'serpents': *Mus* XVI p. 80.

19 N does not follow the distinction, customary in theological usage, between 'Christ' and 'Jesus'.

20 See Schopenhauer's *Parerga und Paralipomena*, vol. II § 109; convincing evidence to support this discovery is given by J. Salaquarda, 'Der Antichrist' in *NS* II (Berlin 1973), pp. 91-136. For N's self-identification as 'Antichrist' see his letter to Meysenbug, end of March 1883.

21 Hans Küng, *On Being a Christian* (London 1976), p. 89.

22 See C. S. Lewis, *Christian Reflections* (London 1967), p. 153.

23 For a full account of N's anti-ecclesiastical and anti-Christian views, see E. Benz, *N's Ideen zur Geschichte des Christentums und der Kirche* (Leiden 1956), and also Karl Jaspers, *N und das Christentum* (Hameln no date).

24 Quoted from W. G. Kümmel, *Die Theologie des Neuen Testaments . . .* (Göttingen 1969), p. 227.

25 Whether N ever read Dostoyevsky's novel is uncertain. See C. A. Miller, 'N's "discovery" of Dostoyevsky', *NS* II (Berlin 1973), pp. 202, 257, and W. Gesemann, 'N's Verhältnis zu Dostoevskij auf dem europäischen Hintergrund der 8oer Jahre', in *Welt der Slawen*, VI (Wiesbaden 1961), pp. 131-46.

26 The phrase is Ernst Bertram's; see *N, Versuch einer Mythologie*, 1929 edn, p. 255; cf. also Fink, *op. cit.*, p. 118.

27 It is first mentioned in his Basle lectures of 1872, *Die vorplatonischen Philosophen*, reprinted in *Mus* IV p. 352.

28 See above, p. 60. Nietzsche does not actually say they occur and recur, etc., but he ridicules the clown who denies such a view of history.

29 See Fink, *op. cit.*, chapter 3 § 4.

30 See J. P. Stern, *Hitler: the Führer and the People* (London, Fontana paperback 1975).

6 Discontinuities

1 In most other contexts these two men are not to be mentioned in the same breath.
2 Lionel Trilling, *The Opposing Self* (London 1955), p. 176.
3 In *Essays in Honour of W. J. M. Mackenzie*, ed. B. Chapman and Potter (Manchester 1974), pp. 69-80.
4 See C. S. Lewis's essay, 'On Ethics', in *Christian Reflections*, ed. cit., esp. pp. 48-52.
5 See above, pp. 19-20.

7 Aesthetic Re-interpretation

1 See E. Heller, *The Poet's Self and the Poem*, chapter 2, 'N in the Waste Land'. A possible reference to *Matt.* xviii is repudiated in Z IV § 18; whether the Greeks had any notion of identifying 'the child' with Wordsworthian innocence, as both N and several of his critics do (rather than with mischievousness and caprice), is another question.
2 Not so Heidegger: see *N* I, pp. 333 ff) and Fink, *op. cit.*, pp. 187 to the end.
3 *WKG* III/2 pp. 369-84. An excerpt from the essay is contained in *The Portable N*, pp. 42-7.
4 In a series of notes written at the time of the essay; see *Mus* VI pp. 18-19.
5 Similarly Hegel derives '*Begriff*' from '*begreifen*'; see *Ästhetik* (Berlin 1955), pp. 136f.
6 See Marx's section on money in the *Paris MSS* (*Ökonomisch-philosophische Manuskripte*) of 1844 (München 1966), pp. 103-7; also Jacques Derrida, 'White Mythology: Metaphor in the Text of Philosophy' in *New Literary History* VI/1 Autumn 1974, pp. 12 ff.
7 See also Heinrich von Staden, 'N and Marx on Greek Art and Literature: Case Studies', *Daedalus*, 1976, p. 89.

8 Once he criticizes the belief 'that man's salvation depends on his insight into the *origin of things*' [D § 44] as against the view of things as they are, yet elsewhere the paramount value of origins remains unchallenged.

9 See Bertram, *op. cit.*, pp. 249-259, chapter 'Anekdote'.

10 '. . . dark premonition': R. M. Rilke, *Die Aufzeichnungen des Malte Laurids Brigge* I (Leipzig 1919), p. 139; for the connection between Rilke's 'ein Mal' and N's 'eternal recurrence' see Erich Heller, *The Disinherited Mind*, pp. 128-30.

11 Ferdinand de Saussure, *Course in General Linguistics* [1915] (New York 1959; London, Fontana paperback, 1974) especially chapter 3; cf. also J. Culler, *Saussure* (London, Fontana paperback, 1976).

12 Did he, one wonders, know Baudelaire's description of the artistic imagination in *Salon de 1859* (see his *Curiosités esthétiques*, ed. Henri Lemaître, Paris 1962, § III p. 321)?

Short Bibliography

C. Andler, *Nietzsche: Sa vie et sa pensée.* 6 vols. Paris 1920-31.

C. A. Bernoulli, *Franz Overbeck und Friedrich Nietzsche: eine Freundschaft.* 2 vols. Jena 1908.

E. Bertram, *Nietzsche: Versuch einer Mythologie.* Berlin 1918, reprinted Bonn 1965.

P. Bridgwater, *Nietzsche in Anglosaxony.* Leicester 1972.

F. Copleston, *Friedrich Nietzsche: Philosopher of Culture.* London/New York 1975.

A. C. Danto, *Nietzsche as Philosopher.* New York 1965.

P. Deussen, *Erinnerungen an Friedrich Nietzsche.* Leipzig 1901.

E. Fink, *Nietzsches Philosophie.* Stuttgart 1960.

I. Frenzel, *Friedrich Nietzsche: an Illustrated Biography.* Indianapolis 1967.

I. Frenzel, *Friedrich Nietzsche in Selbstzeugnissen und Bilddokumenten.* (Rowohlts monographien, 115) Reinbek 1966.

G. Grant, *Time as History.* Toronto 1969.

M. Heidegger, *Nietzsche.* 2 vols. Pfullingen 1961.

M. Heidegger, 'Nietzsches Wort "Gott ist tot" . . .' In *Holzwege,* Frankfurt/Main 1950, 1963.

E. Heller, *The Disinherited Mind* (chapters 'Burckhardt and Nietzsche', 'Nietzsche and Goethe', 'Rilke and Nietzsche'). Cambridge 1952.

E. Heller, *The Artist's Journey into the Interior and Other Essays.* New York, Vintage paperback, 1968.

E. Heller, *The Poet's Self and the Poem* (chapter 'Nietzsche in the Wasteland'). London 1976.

E. Heller, 'The Modern German Mind: the Legacy of Nietzsche'. In *Literary Lectures presented at the Library of Congress.* Washington 1973.

P. Heller, *Dialectics and Nihilism: Essays on Lessing, Nietzsche, Manna and Kafka*. Amherst, Mass. 1966.

R. J. Hollingdale, *Nietzsche: the Man and his Philosophy*. Baton Rouge 1965.

R. L. Howey, *Heidegger and Jaspers on Nietzsche: a Critical Examination of Heidegger's and Jaspers's Interpretations of Nietzsche*. The Hague 1973.

K. Jaspers, *Nietzsche: Einführung in das Verständnis seines Philosophierens*. Berlin 1936. (English translation by C. F. Wallraff and F. J. Schmitz, *Nietzsche: an Introduction to the Understanding of his Philosophical Activity*. Tucson 1965.)

K. Jaspers, *Nietzsche und das Christentum*. Hameln n.d. [1946].

W. Kaufmann, *Nietzsche: Philosopher, Psychologist, Antichrist*. Princeton, 4th edn 1974.

J. Lavrin, *Nietzsche: A Biographical Introduction*. London 1971.

F. A. Lea, *The Tragic Philosopher: A Study of Friedrich Nietzsche*. London 1973.

K. Löwith, *Von Hegel zu Nietzsche. Der revolutionäre Bruch im Denken des neunzehnten Jahrhunderts*. Stuttgart 1964. (English translation by D. E. Green, *From Hegel to Nietzsche*. New York 1967, paperback.)

K. Löwith, 'Nietzsche nach sechzig Jahren'. In *Gesammelte Abhandlungen*, Stuttgart 1960.

F. R. Love, *Young Nietzsche and the Wagnerian Experience*. Chapel Hill 1963.

Thomas Mann, *Nietzsche's Philosophie im Lichte unserer Erfahrung*. Berlin 1948.

J. Nolte, *Wahrheit und Freiheit: Meditationen über Texte aus Friedrich Nietzsche* ... Düsseldorf 1973.

E. F. Podach, *Nietzsches Zusammenbruch*. Heidelberg 1930.

M. S. Silk and J. P. Stern, *Nietzsche on Tragedy*. Cambridge 1983, paperback.

H. M. Wolff, *Friedrich Nietzsche: der Weg zum Nichts*. Bern 1956.

Recent Translations

Beyond Good and Evil: Prelude to a Philosophy of the Future (W.

Kaufmann) New York, Vintage Books (paperback) 1973. (R. J. Hollingdale) Harmondsworth, Penguin Books (paperback) 1973.

The Birth of Tragedy and *The Case of Wagner* [The Wagner Case] (W. Kaufmann) New York, Vintage Books (paperback) 1967.

The Gay Science [The Joyous Science] (W. Kaufmann) New York, Vintage Books (paperback) 1974.

On Genealogy of Morals and *Ecce Homo* (W. Kaufmann and R. J. Hollingdale) New York, Vintage Books (paperback) 1973.

Human, All-Too-Human (2 vols.) New York, Gordon Press 1974.

The Antichrist and *Twilight of the Idols* (R. J. Hollingdale) Harmondsworth, Penguin Books (paperback) 1969.

Thus Spoke Zarathustra (W. Kaufmann) New York, Viking Books (paperback) 1966. (R. J. Hollingdale) Harmondsworth, Penguin Books (paperback) 1969.

The Will to Power (W. Kaufmann and R. J. Hollingdale) New York, Viking Books (paperback) 1968.

Thoughts out of Season (2 vols.) New York, Gordon Press 1974; *Untimely Meditations* (R. J. Hollingdale, intro. J. P. Stern) Cambridge University Press 1983.

The Dawn of Day [Aurora] New York, Gordon Press 1974; *Daybreak: Thoughts on the Prejudices of Morality* (R. J. Hollingdale, intro. Michael Tanner) Cambridge University Press 1982.

The Portable Nietzsche (W. Kaufmann) New York, Viking Books (paperback) 1973. Contains translations of: *Thus Spoke Zarathustra, Twilight of the Idols, The Antichrist* and *Nietzsche contra Wagner*.

A Nietzsche Reader (R. J. Hollingdale) Harmondsworth, Penguin Books (paperback) 1977.

Hitler: The Führer and the People

J. P. Stern

His life, his times, his policies, his strategies, his influence have often been analysed. But rarely is the most elementary question of all raised – how could it happen?

How could a predominantly sober, hard-working, and well-educated population have been persuaded to follow Hitler to the awful abyss of destruction? What was the source of his immense popularity? What was the image projected in his speeches, his writings, and his conversation?

Hitler: The Führer and the People is a compelling attempt to reconstruct the nature of Hitler's political ideology, its roots, logic, and function.

'Who really wants or needs another book on Hitler? The short answer is, when the book is as good and original and brief as Professor Stern's, that we all do.'

Donald G. MacRae, *New Statesman*

'Stern's book is, on all counts, a significant achievement.'

Geoffrey Barraclough, *New York Review of Books*

'. . . an excellent book, all the more so because it concerns itself, via Hitler, with the more general problems of the relationship between society and the individual leader, between ideas and action, between myth and reality.'

Douglas Johnson, *New Society*

'His short book is one of the most remarkable studies of Hitler and Nazism to have appeared.'   Christopher Sykes, *Observer*